MW00791044

COLUMNS

Nikolai Zabolotsky
COLUMNS

Translated by
Dmitri Manin

Introduced by
Darra Goldstein

PUBLICATIONS

2023

Published by Arc Publications,
Nanholme Mill, Shaw Wood Road,
Todmorden OL14 6DA, UK
www.arcpublications.co.uk

978 1911469 15 5
Design by Tony Ward

Cover painting:
Olga Rozanova 'Fire in the Town' 1914

The poems in this book are taken from Zabolotsky's 1958
version of *Columns*, but because of the length of the book, the
publishers decided to omit 16 poems. They are: [from Part I
'Urban Columns'] 'Болезнь' (Sickness), 'На лестницах' (On the
Stairs), 'Купальщики' (Bathers), 'Самовар' (Samova), 'На даче'
(At the Dacha) and 'Начало осени' (Early Autumn); [from Part II
'Mixed Columns'] 'Лицо коня' (A Steed's Face), 'Змеи' (Snakes),
'Вопросы к морю' (Questioning the Sea), 'Поэма дождя' (Poem
of Rain), 'Птицы' (Birds), 'Человек в воде' (A Man in Water),
'Звезды, розы и квадраты' (Stars and Roses and Rectangles),
'Царица мух' (The Queen of the Flies), 'Подводный город' (The
Undersea Town) and 'Школа жуков' (The School of Beetles).

ACKNOWLEDGEMENTS
Translations of 'Immaturity', 'Foxtrot' and 'Vagrant Musicians' (from
the Russian text in the 1929 version of *Columns*) appeared in *Cardinal
Points*, Vol 8 (2018), and translations of 'The Bakery', 'Snowballs', 'On
the Stairs' and 'A Walk' were published in *Delos*, Vol 33, no. 2 (2018).

**Arc 'Visible Poets' Series
Series Editor: Jean Boase-Beier**

CONTENTS

SERIES EDITOR'S NOTE

The 'Visible Poets' series was established in 2000, and set out to challenge the view that translated poetry could or should be read without regard to the process of translation it had undergone. Since then, things have moved on. Today there is more translated poetry available and more debate on its nature, its status, and its relation to its original. We know that translated poetry is neither English poetry that has mysteriously arisen from a hidden foreign source, nor is it foreign poetry that has silently rewritten itself in English. We are more aware that translation lies at the heart of all our cultural exchange; without it, we must remain artistically and intellectually insular.

One of the aims of the series was, and still is, to enrich our poetry with the very best work that has appeared elsewhere in the world. And the poetry-reading public is now more aware than it was at the start of this century that translation cannot simply be done by anyone with two languages. The translation of poetry is a creative act, and translated poetry stands or falls on the strength of the poet-translator's art. For this reason 'Visible Poets' publishes only the work of the best translators, and gives each of them space, in a Preface, to talk about the trials and pleasures of their work.

From the start, 'Visible Poets' books have been bilingual. Many readers will not speak the languages of the original poetry but they, too, are invited to compare the look and shape of the English poems with the originals. Those who can are encouraged to read both. Translation and original are presented side-by-side because translations do not displace the originals; they shed new light on them and are in turn themselves illuminated by the presence of their source poems. By drawing the readers' attention to the act of translation itself, it is the aim of these books to make the work of both the original poets and their translators more visible.

Jean Boase-Beier

...And life flew over like a trough
Crackling and hanging upside down.

To me, these closing lines from Nikolay Zabolotsky's poem 'The Circus' epitomize the spirit of this book: a worldview with no oppositions, no differences between the living and dead, abstract and concrete, naive and sophisticated, artful and artless, meaningful and meaningless, high and low, important and trivial, funny and sad. It's all mixed inseparably (or maybe 'jumbled' is a better word) in this world of ours.

I don't remember when and how I first read *Columns* – probably in my late teens. The poems startled me and stayed with me. Although I only remembered a couple of lines, I could instantly recognize their echoes in other poets.

In 2016 I went to a reading by a Zabolotsky scholar, Igor Loschilov, in Samovar, the local Russian community hub in New York City. For most of the evening, Igor recited poems from *Columns*, and his incredibly artistic reading rekindled my love for them. By that time, I'd been actively translating poetry from English and French into Russian for several years; I'd close-read thousands of lines of English poetry and felt that I was gradually learning to appreciate the way it worked. Of course, on a higher level it works the same way as poetry in any other language, but I'm talking about the mechanics: the rhythms, the sounds, the idiosyncratically English turns of phrase.

Before that time, I was adamant about never even attempting to translate anything into a non-native language. But then, suddenly, I felt an irresistible urge to try. Just to make sure nothing good would come out of it, of course. *Columns* presented a nice challenge. Besides, I was pretty sure that English poetry hadn't seen anything like these poems yet, so it was an interesting opportunity to create something new. And I thought that Zabolotsky's strange new language could hide my inevitable accent. That last part, of course, was a delusion; things don't work that way. Any strangeness has to be firmly grounded in the conventional language to be convincing, just like the distorted figures in a modernist painting can only be convincing if the artist knew how to draw a realistic figure in the first place.

Zabolotsky was a co-founder of a small and short-lived group called OBERIU. He formed it in 1927 with two other extraordinary poets of avant-garde persuasion, Daniil Kharms and Alexander Vvedensky. The name is ostensibly an acronym for 'Association for Real Art', except that the final 'U' is left unexplained in a touch of absurdism so characteristic of this group.

As often happens, the group founders were very different poets, and it's hard to define what it was that united them, other than their opposition to other groups that abounded in this time of swirling and bubbling literary life. Perhaps their keen sense of the tragic absurdity of life in post-revolutionary Russia was one of the most important defining features. The world was coming apart, and they engaged in a hopeless attempt to put it back together with the magic of words, where crumbling meanings were held together with the cement of sound. Of course, they wrote manifestos, incomprehensible as most such manifestos are, being just a continuation of poetic practices by other means rather than a product of a detached analytical mind.

Avant-garde poets often draw some of their inspiration from their contemporary art. Thus, Language poets mingled with Abstract Expressionist painters and Soviet post-war underground poets with Conceptualist artists. The Oberiuts felt a strong affinity with French Cubist painting and similar Russian art movements, and this can explain many features of their poetry, especially their deliberate artlessness, childlike naivete. Like avant-garde artists, the Oberiuts were breaking free from established norms to refresh the perception of the world. I am even tempted to treat the seemingly unmotivated changes of verb tense that frequently disrupt the flow of their poems as verbal counterparts to the broken planes of Cubism.

The poetry of *Columns* is very visual, palpable, concrete. Many of the poems are vignettes of 1920s urban life, but even the philosophical poems abound with vividly concrete images, and, conversely, the narrative poems keep zooming out to cosmic scales, as in 'A Wedding' (p. 51):

There, at the heart of all existence,
A showy fish pie takes the stage.

Probably one of the most noticeable features in the poetics of *Columns* is strange metaphors and similes which go far out on a limb, but stop short of absurdity: eyeballs falling down like kettlebells, grapes dancing in the footballer's windpipe, pies ripening like golden thoroughbreds and so on.

Many poems from *Columns* have been translated previously by Daniel Weissbort,[1] and then, revised and expanded, in 1999. In his 'Translator's Preface' to the 1999 edition[2], Weissbort explains his approach as "steer[ing] a course between the Scylla of domestication and Charybdis of foreignizing, training myself to be on the lookout for instances where conventionalism had nudged me into toning down images".

Instead of venturing into the arid landscape of translation theory, where terms like 'foreignization' belong, let's take a look at a short example that will hopefully explain my approach. I picked the following two lines from the poem describing "white nights" in St. Petersburg, those midsummer nights when the sun dips so briefly behind the horizon in this northern city that it never really gets dark, a dizzying season of love and yearnings. Weissbort has two rather different versions of these lines:

here wine-slurred laughter soars
like a parrot up in flight;
(1971, p. 17)

parrot-like, from mouth to mouth,
drunken laughter loops, uncouth;
(1999, p. 25)

If one had to guess what the original looked like (a translator's bad habit), a good bet would be something

---

[1] *Scrolls*, (London: Jonathan Cape, 1971)
[2] *Selected Poems of Nikolay Zabolotsky*, (Manchester: Carcanet Press, 1999)

like "wine-slurred laughter flies like a parrot". Indeed, the original lines read, in a super-literal translation,

here, from wine unrecognizable,
flies laughter parrot-like.

Or, in something approaching normal English, "Laughter, made unrecognizable by wine, flies around here parrot-like". There are a couple of lexical nuances, though. First, there are two words for "laughter" in Russian: one neutral, and the other one, *khokhot*, used here, denotes a more violent, roaring kind of laughter. Second, Russian distinguishes verbs for one-time action from verbs for repeated or habitual action, and the verb for "fly" here is the latter kind. That's why I wrote "flies around", rather than simply "flies". Third, Russian has a lot of ways to express a simile, and the one used here (for "parrot-like") utilizes the instrumental case of the noun "parrot". This kind of simile sounds especially forceful, because it doesn't use any auxiliary words such as "like" or "as". We could approximate it in English with something like "laughter parrot-flies", except it's not a common model (though wouldn't it be nice if it were?)

My description would be incomplete without mentioning the formal aspects of the couplet. These lines are written in iambic tetrameter, the meter of Wordsworth's "I wandered lonely as a cloud". They rhyme, the rhyming words being "unrecognizable" and "parrot". They are also shot through with additional sound echoes, for example, "flies" also chimes with "parrot". The dominant vowel sound is a repeated "ah", while the word for "laughter" is foregrounded by carrying the only stressed "oh".

Finally, let's zoom out from sounds and words to the level of images. Typically for Zabolotsky, he takes something abstract – laughter in this case – and makes it a solid, palpable thing, even a living thing, a parrot. Laughter is seen as flying between people like a bird, but also echoing like a parrot, and even resembling the sharp cries of macaws or parakeets. But more than just a poetic simile, the word "unrecognizable" presents this as a magical transformation. From the commonsense point of view, it's not a big stretch to liken laughter to a parrot cry, and even likening laughter to a flitting bird itself is not a revolutionary metaphor. But to say that laughter is so thoroughly transformed into a parrot that it's not recognizable as laughter any more, now *that* is daring. The rhyming position of the word "unrecognizable" further emphasizes its crucial role.

Coming back to Weissbort's versions, isn't it curious that the only part of the original that is consistently missing in both is precisely the word "unrecognizable"? In his renderings, the hyperbolic transformation of laughter into a parrot is reduced to a fairly commonplace metaphor. For my purposes, this omission is much more significant than his adding extra words to make the lines rhyme or for other reasons. Here's the way I have translated the couplet:

And bursts of wine-transfigured laughter,
Turned parrots, flit around and flutter.

I didn't keep the word "unrecognizable" literally, but transferred its thrust to two other words: "transfigured" and "turned". Perhaps I still smoothed it out a little by replacing laughter with bursts of laughter. I felt that having uncountable laughter turn into a countable parrot would sound more jarring in English than it does in Russian, which has no articles.

Of course, there's no one true way to do translation. The way one translates a poem depends on the translator's goals and aspirations. My own work is driven by the desire to share: to share the thrill of reading with my reader, but also to share in the thrill of writing the poem with its author. Most, if not all, translators aspire to some form of equivalence, be it creating a text that perfectly matches the original poem in another language, or creating a reading experience that perfectly matches the experience of the source-language reader. When I consider what my ideal translation might be, I tend more to the latter form of equivalence. However, it is not as straightforward as it seems at first blush.

To begin with, when we say 'source-language reader', who exactly do we have in mind? Reader experiences vary widely across contemporaneous readers depending on their cultural backgrounds and personal preferences. They also change a lot as time passes, and what began as a daring innovation becomes established in the canon or sinks into obscurity, inspires imitations or remains a glorious dead end. Things become even murkier when the reader comes from a different literary tradition. So, much as I'd like to transplant my reading experience directly into the mind of my reader, I have to admit that this is impossible and settle for the next best thing. What this next best thing is, depends on the translator. One can, for instance, try to create a poem that would function in the target literary tradition in the same way as the original functioned in its native literature. (Incidentally, this could be said to be the essence of the 'domesticating' approach.)

My approach is different. My ideal translation has the same effect on the target-language reader as if the language barrier was magically removed, the original text became fully accessible to the reader, but both the text and the reader remained firmly rooted in their respective literary traditions. In other words, I don't try to either move the reader closer to the text or the text to the reader, but simply remove the opaque screen between them. Of course, some overtones, allusions and meanings will elude the reader. But it would be naive to assume that an average native speaker necessarily gets all the original overtones and allusions of a 100-years-old poem. They don't, but they also bring in new shades of meanings and see echoes of things that didn't exist when the poem was written. Likewise, a reader from a different culture will, if we are lucky, read things into the poem. This is, after all, what keeps good literature alive.

Dmitri Manin

When *Columns* (*Stolbtsy*), a slim volume of poems written by an unknown young poet named Nikolai Zabolotsky appeared in 1929, it took the Leningrad literary world by storm. Zabolotsky was not part of the city's artistic elite; he had arrived in Petrograd (as Leningrad was then called) from the provinces only eight years earlier, unschooled in cosmopolitan ways and distant from the cultural traditions of the Acmeists or Symbolists. Yet within less than a decade after his arrival, Zabolotsky's startlingly original poetry had catapulted him into prominence. His artistic vision was in part spurred by the dismal conditions he encountered in his adopted city. The deprivations of the Revolution (1917) and Civil War (1917-22) years had taken their toll. Yet even as Zabolotsky subsisted mainly on black bread and boiled water, his imagination was freed from the confines of accustomed perception by the city's very starkness. The air itself seemed rarefied: commonplace objects stood out vividly and sharply defined, no longer characterized primarily by their use or by the observer's expectations, but as profound things in themselves. For the young poet, these new perceptions seemed full of sudden beauty and, potentially, truth.

Columns sold out its edition of 1200 copies almost immediately. The volume included twenty-two poems written between 1926 and 1928 that carry the reader on a strange circuit of Leningrad, a city caught in the vulgarities and confusion of the New Economic Policy (NEP) period. The tour begins during the White Night of a Leningrad summer before heading into a bar called the Red Bavaria. Proceeding through the city, the reader encounters a soccer game, a marketplace, a bakery, a fishmonger, and more. If markets are conventionally presented as wonderlands of enticing produce, Zabolotsky shows his readers the market's actual essence, its blood and guts: "Meat hangs, ruled by the butcher's ax, / A gaping hole, red on the racks, / And sausages, like bloody bowels, / Hiss on the grill full of hot coals."

We continue on past the flea markets near Leningrad's Bypass Canal and stop to listen to street musicians performing in the courtyards. One of the most raucous stops is at a wedding, where the focus is not on the beauty of the bride but on the vulgarity of the feast:

A bulging flock of fleshy dames
Sit round; their feathers are like flames,
A balding ermine crown that frames
Their ample bosoms dimly sheens
In the sweat of centenarian queens.
Their breath coarse with unsated passions,
They munch on glutinous confections,
They let their guts loose from the laces,
And press close to the plates and vases.

Zabolotsky uses displacement, odd metaphors, and irregular syntax to shatter conventional modes of perception and force us to consider people and objects anew. The world portrayed in the poems of *Columns* seems to exist outside of time and space. Waking and dream states, the real and the unreal, merge as Zabolotsky jars his reader into different states of consciousness. The result is a verbal grotesque akin to that described by the avant-garde theatre director Vsevolod Meyerhold: "The main thing in the grotesque is the artist's constant striving to lead the viewer out of the plane he has only just reached and onto another which he didn't expect." Even as Zabolotsky shifts planes, startling his reader from accustomed perceptions, he fixes the images in the reader's mind by making them concrete: as the loud laughter in 'White Night' flies fleetingly through the air, Zabolotsky makes it visible and very nearly palpable by likening it to a parrot.

In the official declaration of the poetic group OBERIU with which he was associated, Zabolotsky explained his approach: "N. Zabolotsky is a poet of bare, concrete figures moved right up to the eyes of the observer." His method may be compared to the cinematic technique of montage developed around that time by Sergei Eisenstein, whereby quick and heterogeneous shots of life are rapidly juxtaposed upon the screen. Taken together, the scenes jar the viewers into perceiving the world in a new way by creating an integrated picture that is all the more vivid for having been dissected before them. Zabolotsky's technique in *Columns* often approaches montage in its use of abrupt juxtapositions and dissolves. Such displacements challenge the reader to participate in the poetic process.

Born on a farm near Kazan in 1903, Nikolai Alekseyevich Zabolotsky grew up in a series of remote provincial villages before escaping at the age of ten to the relative cosmopolitanism of the town of Urzhum. There he studied at the local, practical high school before leaving in 1920 for Moscow, where he enrolled in the Faculty of History and Philology at the First University of Moscow. Unable to find enough food to sustain him, Zabolotsky returned to his family and the relative plenty of Urzhum in March 1921, but by August of that year he left for Petrograd, where he entered the Herzen Pedagogical Institute. And there his life as a poet began.

After completing his studies in 1925, Zabolotsky encountered Daniil Kharms and Aleksandr Vvedensky, two remarkable poets who helped lift him out of obscurity. He began writing poetry in earnest and in 1927 accepted a job in the Children's Section of the State Publishing House, working alongside Kharms, Vvedensky, and other innovative writers. The job proved a lifeline for them, if only temporarily, as independent literary life grew increasingly constrained in the late 1920s. Children's literature provided income and an outlet for the writers' talents when they could no longer easily publish their work for adults.

Around 1927 Zabolotsky began making public appearances with Kharms, Vvedensky and other young Leningrad poets with whom he formed a group called OBERIU, the Association for Real Art. The group performed regularly at Leningrad's House of the Press in staged, theatrical performances. In January 1928 the OBERIU published a declaration championing the social utility of poetry. Art was not to stand above the masses, but to be accessible to them, transforming them through a new and revolutionary perception of the world. They were the "poets of a new perception of the world and a new art, builders of a new poetic language, creators of a new perception of life and its objects." Like other modernists, they sought to transform the world through the word and – like the Futurists before them – make the word itself new and elementary. This collision of word and object they termed *predmetnost'* (concreteness). In coining this term, they reacted against the *bespredmetnost'* (non-objectivity or lack of concreteness) of much of avant-garde art. To underscore their rootedness in the concrete and quotidian, they would haul an actual cupboard onto stage during performances.

Zabolotsky's early poetry is often playful, even when it deals with existential ideas. The resulting ambiguity of tone confounded his critics, many of whom failed to understand the essential irony of his vision. The response to *Columns* was immediate and strong. While the noted critic Nikolai Stepanov likened Zabolotsky's verbal art to the visual: "A compulsiveness, an almost *lubok* [woodblock] vividness of the word is one of the principles of his poetic method," other critics reacted with vituperation. Four reviewers in leading publications censured Zabolotsky for what they perceived as his depiction of a timeless, inescapable vulgarity. They insisted that he should have used his considerable talent to extol the rebuilding of society, the great theme of the early Soviet era.

From that point on, ideological attacks against Zabolotsky began to appear sporadically in the press. He remained fairly oblivious to them, absorbed as he was in writing his long dramatic poem 'The Triumph of Agriculture', two sections of which he managed to publish in late 1929. By the time he completed the poem in 1930, however, his position was so problematic that he could not find a publisher for several years. In 1933, when the poem finally appeared in its entirety in the journal *The Star*, it was immediately assailed as a mockery of collectivization (the campaign to organize private farms into large, state-run entities). The negative reviews of 'The Triumph of Agriculture' frequently included *Columns* in their indictments. And so Zabolotsky's second book of poems was suppressed, even though the galley proofs were ready for publication.

Zabolotsky's situation grew increasingly tenuous. On 19 March 1938, he was arrested and taken to Leningrad's Remand Prison, where he endured interrogation and torture. That August he was transferred to the notorious Kresty Prison and on September 2 was accused of belonging to a subversive writers' organization. He was sentenced without trial to five years in a labour camp for "Trotskyite counter-revolutionary activity." After his release, Zabolotsky wrote about his ordeal in *The Story of My Imprisonment*, which remained unpublished during his lifetime. His description of his wintertime transit to Siberia, in a barely heated freight wagon, reveals him as still very much the author of *Columns*, a poet ever cognizant of the grotesque:

> From time to time the authorities appeared in the wagon to carry out a check.
> So as to verify the numbers they made us all go on to one ledge of planks. At a special command we had to crawl across a board to the other ledge, and they counted us as we did so. The picture is as vivid before me as if it were happening now: black with soot, beards sprouting, we crawl one after the other on all fours like monkeys across the board, lit by the dim glow of lanterns, while a semi-literate guard holds us at rifle point and counts and counts away, getting muddled in his tricky calculations.

Zabolotsky had been sent to a settlement in the Russian Far East near the newly built city of Komsomolsk-on-Amur, where he laboured at various sites for the full five years of his term. His scheduled release in March 1943 was postponed due to World War II; instead, he was transferred to the Altai Region of Siberia, where he was compelled to work in a mine extracting soda, which shattered his health. He was released into exile on 18 August 1944. His wife and two children joined him, and in March 1945 the family moved to Karaganda in central Kazakhstan. Zabolotsky was finally allowed to return to Moscow in January 1946, thus ending nearly eight years of imprisonment and exile.

Post-camp life brought its own difficulties. For one thing, Zabolotsky could not shake off his fear. When friends admiringly quoted from *Columns*, he felt terrified; he didn't want to talk about the literary work that had led to his arrest. Even though Zabolotsky was able to publish two more volumes of verse, he lived under constant threat of rearrest and was not formally rehabilitated during his lifetime. When, in 1958, Zabolotsky was awarded the Order of Labour of the Red Banner, he accepted this symbol of governmental approbation and sat for an official photograph. But when he returned home, he methodically cut out his decorated chest from the photograph, until only his solemn face remained.

Nikolai Zabolotsky died of a heart attack on 14 October 1958. Over the last decade of his life, he largely abandoned the modernist experiments of his early, urban poetry and turned instead to meditations on nature in lyrical, philosophical verse. For many decades the last link in the Russian Futurist tradition, Zabolotsky was also the first significant poet to come of age in the Soviet era. His life was both tragic and emblematic. How fortunate we are that Dmitri Manin has undertaken to convey the daring strangeness of Zabolotsky's early verse to an Anglophone audience. Although Manin modestly presents himself as a non-native speaker of English, the linguistic challenge serves him well as he enters into Zabolotsky's universe of unexpected associations. He surely succeeds in his aim to "amaze and thrill the English reader" in his excellent rendering of Zabolotsky's verse.

Darra Goldstein

COLUMNS

I

ГОРОДСКИЕ СТОЛБЦЫ

БЕЛАЯ НОЧЬ

Гляди: не бал, не маскарад,
Здесь ночи ходят невпопад,
Здесь от вина неузнаваем,
Летает хохот попугаем.
Здесь возле каменных излучин
Бегут любовники толпой,
Один горяч, другой измучен,
А третий книзу головой.
Любовь стенает под листами,
Она меняется местами,
То подойдет, то отойдет…
А музы любят круглый год.

Качалась Невка у перил,
Вдруг барабан заговорил –
Ракеты, выстроившись кругом,
Вставали в очередь. Потом
Они летели друг за другом,
Вертя бенгальским животом.

Качали кольцами деревья,
Спадали с факелов отрепья
Густого дыма. А на Невке
Не то сирены, не то девки,
Но нет, сирены, – на заре,
Все в синеватом серебре,
Холодноватые, но звали
Прижаться к палевым губам

I

URBAN COLUMNS

THE WHITE NIGHT

Look: not a masquerade, nor a feast,
Nights wander here, lost in the mist,
And bursts of wine-transfigured laughter,
Turned parrots, flit around and flutter.
And here, among the stone-clad piers
A motley flock of lovers wheels:
One languished and another fierce,
Another yet, head over heels.
Love moans beneath the shade of leaves,
Trades places, shifts, arrives and leaves,
Now here, now nowhere to be found…
But Muses love us all year round.

The Nevka swayed beneath the railing,
And all at once drums started rumbling,
Firecrackers lined up in a ring
Waiting in turn like coloured jellies.
Then they went soaring in a string,
And twirled their sparkling Bengal bellies.

Trees waved their rings on the embankment,
And torches shed rough shreds of thickened
Smoke. On the Nevka before sunrise,
Sirens – or maybe girls – no, sirens
They were – bathed in the silver blue
Of dawn, they beckoned us to glue
Our lips to their lips, pallid petals.
They called, cold in the morning light,

21

И неподвижным, как медали.
Обман с мечтами пополам!

Я шел сквозь рощу. Ночь легла
Вдоль по траве, как мел бела.
Торчком кусты над нею встали
В ножнах из разноцветной стали,
И тосковали соловьи
Верхом на веточке. Казалось,
Они испытывали жалость,
Как неспособные к любви.

А там, вдали, где желтый бакен
Подкарауливал шутих,
На корточках привстал Елагин,
Ополоснулся и затих:
Он в этот раз накрыл двоих.

Вертя винтом, бежал моторчик
С музыкой томной по бортам.
К нему навстречу, рожи скорчив,
Несутся лодки тут и там.
Он их толкнет – они бежать.
Бегут, бегут, потом опять
Идут, задорные, навстречу.
Он им кричит: "Я искалечу!"
Они уверены, что нет...

И всюду сумасшедший бред.
Листами сонными колышим,
Он льется в окна, липнет к крышам,
Вздымает дыбом волоса...
И ночь, подобно самозванке,

Silent and motionless like medals.
Oh, half delusion and half lie!

I walked among the trees. The night
Stretched out over the grass, chalk-white.
The shrubs stood upright overhead,
In iridescent metal clad.
And nightingales grieved in the grove
Astride their perches. They appeared
So heartbroken, as though they feared
They were unqualified to love.

And out there, where a yellow buoy
Was catching fireworks on the river,
Elagin* squatted in a ploy:
It splashed itself and went for cover,
This time it caught a pair of lovers.

A motorboat rolling its screw
Spilled languid music from the deck,
But dinghies, making faces, flew
Towards it and behind its back.
It jogs them, they scurry away,
Then circle back into the fray
And cross its course, impudent fellows.
"I'll get and cripple you!" – it bellows,
But that is just a joke to them…

And all's rife with delirium.
It's fanned by drowsy leaves and boughs,
It clings to roofs, through windows ploughs
And sends a shiver down the spines...
Night, the impostor, above all

* Elagin or Yelagin is an island on the Nevka river in St. Petersburg.

Открыв молочные глаза,
Качается в спиртовой банке
И просится на небеса.

1926

Вечерний бар

В глуши бутылочного рая,
Где пальмы высохли давно,
Под электричеством играя,
В бокале плавало окно.
Оно, как золото, блестело,
Потом садилось, тяжелело,
Над ним пивной дымок вился…
Но это рассказать нельзя.

Звеня серебряной цепочкой,
Спадает с лестницы народ,
Трещит картонною сорочкой,
С бутылкой водит хоровод.
Сирена бледная за стойкой
Гостей попотчует настойкой,
Скосит глаза, придет, уйдет,
Потом с гитарой наотлет
Она поет, поет о милом,
Как милого она любила,
Как ласков к телу и жесток,
Впивался шелковый шнурок,
Как по стаканам висла виски,

With her wide-open milky eyes
Floats in a jar of alcohol
And begs to be taken to the skies.

   1926

THE LATE-NIGHT BAR

In the backlands of bottle heaven
Where palms had withered long ago
A window in a wineglass, cloven,
Floated in the electric glow.
A beery haze above it hung,
The window settled down and clung,
Solidified and shone like gold…
But this has to be left untold.

Amid the jingle of silver chains,
Amid the cardboard shirt-fronts' rattle
Down from the stairs the drinker rains
And pirouettes around the bottle.
Pale in the face, a siren nests
Behind the bar and tends the guests;
She squints and goes away, comes back
With a guitar around her neck
And sings. She sings about her lover,
The only one she'd love forever,
About the silken cord* stretched tight ,
Its cruel caress and tender bite,
And whiskey hanging in the shot,

* A reference to a song in the genre of "cruel romance", popular at the time, "Silken Cord" (https://www.youtube.com/watch?v=dW-aDoI31bg).

25

Как из разбитого виска
Измученную грудь обрызгав,
Он вдруг упал. Была тоска,
И все, о чем она ни пела,
Легло в бокал белее мела.

Мужчины тоже все кричали,
Они качались по столам,
По потолкам они качали
Бедлам с цветами пополам.
Один рыдает, толстопузик,
Другой кричит: "Я – Иисусик,
Молитесь мне, я на кресте,
В ладонях гвозди и везде!"
К нему сирена подходила,
И вот, тарелки оседлав,
Бокалов бешеный конклав
Зажегся, как паникадило.

Глаза упали, точно гири,
Бокал разбили, вышла ночь.
И жирные автомобили,
Схватив под мышки Пикадилли,
Легко откатывали прочь.
А за окном в глуши времен
Блистал на мачте лампион.

Там Невский в блеске и тоске,
В ночи переменивший краски,
От сказки был на волоске,
Ветрами вея без опаски.
И как бы яростью объятый,
Через туман, тоску, бензин,

About the scarlet whisk that shot
From temples to the anguished breast
When he fell promptly. Yearnings pressed,
And all the singing and the talk
Settled in the wineglass, white as chalk.

The men all shouted too and squabbled,
And swayed the ceiling in the room,
And at the tables swung and wobbled
And mixed the bedlam with the bloom.
One man, pot-bellied, sobs and wheezes,
Another clamours: "I'm a Jesus,
Nails in my hands and everywhere,
Here on the cross I hear your prayer!"
The siren from the bar drew near;
Astride the plates a wild conclave
Of glasses flared like in the nave
A grave and pompous chandelier.

Eyeballs fell down like kettlebells,
Shattered the glass, and night emerged.
Fat limousines with glistening grills
Grabbed Piccadilly* by the gills
And slowly into the darkness lurched.
A paper lantern on a mast
Shone in the thickness of the past.

At arm's reach from a fairy tale,
The Nevsky sat, all gloom and glitter,
It sent along its fearless gale,
Its colours shimmered, sweet to bitter.
And there a winged and furious sphere
Through haze and gloom and gasoline

* Here, a luxury cinema theater on the Nevsky avenue.

Над башней рвался шар крылатый
И имя "Зингер" возносил.

1926

ФУТБОЛ

Ликует форвард на бегу.
Теперь ему какое дело!
Недаром сомкнуто в дугу
Его стремительное тело.
Как плащ, летит его душа,
Ключица стукается звонко
О перехват его плаща.
Танцует в ухе перепонка,
Танцует в горле виноград,
И шар перелетает ряд.

Его хватают наугад,
Его отравою поят,
Но башмаков железный ряд
Ему страшнее во сто крат.
Назад!

Свалились в кучу беки,
Опухшие от сквозняка,
Но к ним через моря и реки,
Просторы, площади, снега,
Расправив пышные доспехи

Hitched up on an exalted spire
Spelled "Singer"* high above the scene.

   1926

FOOTBALL

The forward runs triumphantly.
What does he care? It's all the same!
Arched like a bow from head to knee
Is his impetuous, furious frame.
His soul flies trailing like a drape,
His clavicle cheerfully clinks
Against the buckle of his cape,
Within his ear the membrane winks,
The grapes deep in his windpipe dance,
The leather orb soars over the stands.

It goes from hands to bustling hands,
It gets suffused with pestilence,
But most of all it apprehends
The iron bane of boots! Back thence
It comes!

The backs pile up and shiver
From chilly draft, but bound their way –
Across the sea, across the river,
Across the steppe, the snow, the rain –
Spreading the splendour of its armour,

* A logo of the Singer Sewing Machine Company on top of the building next to the bar being described. The building belonged to Singer
before the revolution.

29

И накренясь в меридиан,
Несется шар.

В душе у форварда пожар,
Гремят, как сталь, его колена,
Но уж из горла бьет фонтан,
Он падает, кричит: "Измена!"
А шар вертится между стен,
Дымится, пучится, хохочет,
Глазок сожмет: "Спокойной ночи!"
Глазок откроет: "Добрый день!"
И форварда замучить хочет.

Четыре гола пали в ряд,
Над ними трубы не гремят,
Их сосчитал и тряпкой вытер
Меланхолический голкипер
И крикнул ночь. Приходит ночь.
Бренча алмазною заслонкой,
Она вставляет черный ключ
В атмосферическую лунку.
Открылся госпиталь. Увы,
Здесь форвард спит без головы.

Над ним два медные копья
Упрямый шар веревкой вяжут,
С плиты загробная вода
Стекает в ямки вырезные,
И сохнет в горле виноград.
Спи, форвард, задом наперед!

Спи, бедный форвард!
Над землею
Заря упала, глубока,
Танцуют девочки с зарею
У голубого ручейка.

Heeling to the meridian
Hurtles the sphere.

The forward's heart is now on fire,
His knees of stainless metal rumble,
His throat spouts forth a fountain,
He cries out "treason!" in a tumble.
The orb whirls round and dashes through,
It steams, puffs out, cackles with spite,
It shuts an eye: "Good night, good night!"
It winks an eye: "How do you do!"
And racks the forward with a fight.

Four goals have fallen in a row,
But no victorious trumpets blow,
Only the melancholic goalie
Keeps count, then wipes them solemnly
And calls the night. The night arrives.
Her diamond shutters softly tinkle,
She draws her pitch-black pin and drives
It in the atmospheric pinhole.
The hospital lights up. Alas!
There sleeps the forward, head amiss.

Two brazen spears crossed over him
Hobble the stubborn orb with ropes,
Sepulchral water from the tombstone
Drips through the carved-out ornament,
The windpipe grapes have shrunk and withered.
Sleep, forward, sleep from now on backward!

Sleep tight!
Already, deep and wide,
The dawn above the earth has set,
Girls dance their cheerful dance beside
A skipping sky-blue rivulet.

Все так же вянут на покое
В лиловом домике обои,
Стареет мама с каждым днем…
Спи, бедный форвард!
Мы живем.

    1926

Офорт

И грянул на весь оглушительный зал:
"Покойник из царского дома бежал!"

Покойник по улицам гордо идет,
Его постояльцы ведут под уздцы,
Он голосом трубным молитву поет
И руки ломает наверх.
Он в медных очках, перепончатых рамах,
Переполнен до горла подземной водой.
Над ним деревянные птицы со стуком
Смыкают на створках крыла.
А кругом громобой, цилиндров бряцанье
И курчавое небо, а тут –
Городская коробка с расстегнутой дверью
И за стеклышком – розмарин.

    1927

ИГРА В СНЕЖКИ

В снегу кипит большая драка.
Как легкий бог, летит собака.

Still in the house with lilac shades
In peace and calm wallpaper fades,
Your mother ages as days pass…
Sleep, forward!
Sleep, survived by us.

    1926

AN ETCHING

And rolled through the thunderous hall, echoing:
"The dead man has fled from the house of the king!"

The dead man triumphantly strolls down the streets,
The inmates lead him, bridle over their arms,
He trumpets a prayer in his resonant voice
Wringing his hands to the skies.
He wears brass-rimmed spectacles, membranous frames,
Subterranean water fills him to the brim.
And over his head wooden birds bring together
Their loudly clacking hinged wings.
There's rumbling around, there's clanging of top hats,
All the heavens in curls – but below
Is an urban rectangle with the door unfastened,
And behind glass, a rosemary bush.

    1927

SNOWBALLS

Amid the snow rages a fight.
A god-like dog is stretched in flight.

Мальчишка бьет врага в живот.
На елке тетерев живет.
Уж ледяные свищут бомбы.
Уж вечер. В зареве снега.
В сугробах роя катакомбы,
Мальчишки лезут на врага.
Один, задрав кривые ноги,
Скатился с горки, а другой
Воткнулся в снег, а двое новых,
Мохнатых, скорченных, багровых,
Сцепились вместе, бьются враз,
Но деревянный ножик спас.

Закат погас. И день остановился.
И великаном подошел шершавый конь.
Мужик огромной тушею своей
Сидел в стропилах крашеных саней,
И в медной трубке огонек дымился.

Бой кончился. Мужик не шевелился.

1928

Часовой

На карауле ночь густеет.
Стоит, как башня, часовой.
В его глазах одервенелых
Четырехгранный вьется штык.
Тяжеловесны и крылаты,
Знамена пышные полка,
Как золотые водопады,
Пред ним свисают с потолка.
Там пролетарий на стене

A boy gives gut blows to his foe.
Up in the fir tree two grouse crow.
The air whines with the icy bombs.
The snow glows red. The sun is setting.
The boys push through snow catacombs
Onto the foe, shouting and sweating.
One tumbles down a frozen slide,
His crooked legs up, and another
Is stuck in snow; then two more rush,
Contorted, shaggy, ruddy-blushed,
And get entangled in a fray.
A wooden knife, though, saved the day.

The sunset burned out. The day ceased to pass.
A giant shadow, a rough-hewn horse drew close.
The driver sat still in the painted sled,
His mammoth bulk looming above its bed,
And smoke swirled up from his pipe's blackened brass.

The fighting stopped. The man was motionless.

   1928

THE SENTRY

The night grows denser on his watch.
The sentry stands still as a tower.
And in his numb and wooden eyes
His tetrahedral bayonet swirls.
Before him, pompously unreeling
Heavy fold upon heavy fold,
His regiment's banners from the ceiling
Hang like a cataract of gold.
A proletarian on the wall,

Гремит, играя при луне,
Там вой кукушки полковой
Угрюмо тонет за стеной.
Тут белый домик вырастает
С квадратной башенкой вверху,
На стенке девочка витает,
Дудит в прозрачную трубу.
Уж к ней сбегаются коровы
С улыбкой бледной на губах…
А часовой стоит впотьмах
В шинели конусообразной,
Над ним звезды пожарик красный
И серп заветный в головах.
Вот в щели каменные плит
Мышиные просунулися лица,
Похожие на треугольники из мела,
С глазами траурными по бокам.
Одна из них садится у окошка
С цветочком музыки в руке.
А день в решетку пальцы тянет,
Но не достать ему знамен.
Он напрягается и видит:
Стоит, как башня, часовой,
И пролетарий на стене
Хранит волшебное становье.
Ему знамена – изголовье,
А штык ружья: война – войне.
И день доволен им вполне.

1927

Moonlit, trumpets his thunderous call,
The unit cuckoo's sullen drone
Behind the wall sinks like a stone.
A whitewashed house rises from nowhere,
Crowned with a tall, right-angled turret,
Above the wall a young girl hovers
And blows into a transparent trumpet;
Already cows come running to her,
The smile on their pale lips is fickle...
The sentry stands guard in his conical
Trench coat, amid the midnight dark;
Blessed by the red star's raging spark
Above, and by the cherished sickle.
Between the flagstones in the cracks,
Mouse faces suddenly appear
Resembling white triangles made of chalk
With their sepulchral eyes set in the sides.
And one of them settles beside the window,
A flower of music in its hand.
The day reaches its fingers through
The bars, but falls short of the banners.
It strains to see and can discern
The sentry standing like a tower,
The proletarian on the wall
Guarding the magic bivouac.
The golden banners have his back,
His rifle is a war on war.
And the day approves of him therefore.

   1927

НОВЫЙ БЫТ

Восходит солнце над Москвой,
Старухи бегают с тоской:
Куда, куда идти теперь?
Уж Новый Быт стучится в дверь!
Младенец, выхолен и крупен,
Сидит в купели, как султан.
Прекрасный поп поет, как бубен,
Паникадилом осиян.
Прабабка свечку зажигает,
Младенец крепнет и мужает
И вдруг, шагая через стол,
Садится прямо в комсомол.

И время двинулось быстрее,
Стареет папенька-отец,
И за окошками в аллее
Играет сваха в бубенец.
Ступни младенца стали шире,
От стали ширится рука.
Уж он сидит в большой квартире,
Невесту держит за рукав.
Приходит поп, тряся ногами,
В ладошке мощи бережет,
Благословить желает стенки,
Невесте крестик подарить.
"Увы, – сказал ему младенец, –
Уйди, уйди, кудрявый поп,
Я – новой жизни ополченец,
Тебе ж один остался гроб!"
Уж поп тихонько плакать хочет,
Стоит на лестнице, бормочет,
Не зная, чем себе помочь.
Ужель идти из дома прочь?

THE NEW LIFE

The sun mounts in the Moscow sky,
Old women run around and cry:
Nowhere to go, not anymore,
When the New Life knocks on the door!
An infant, pampered, plump and clean,
Sits like a sultan in the font.
A priest, decked like a tambourine,
Under the candles leads a chant.
A great-grandmother lights up candles,
The infant grows, matures, and straddles
The dinner table, ready to stroll
Right over to the Komsomol.

The time speeds up, now in full stride,
His father grows old and unwell,
And in a tree-lined lane outside
The matchmaker jingles her bell.
The infant's foot gets broad and flat,
Steel makes his hand sturdy and wide.
He sits now in a spacious flat
And holds the sleeve of his new bride.
The priest comes in and wobbles his legs,
He cups saint relics in his hand,
And he desires to bless these walls
And give the bride a pendant cross.
"Alas," – the infant says – "Steer clear
Of me, go back, you curly priest.
I am the new life's volunteer,
And you are as good as deceased!"
The priest holds back unwelcome tears,
Stands muttering something on the stairs,
He doesn't know what to do:
Was he just rudely bid adieu?

Но вот знакомые явились,
Завод пропел: "Ура! Ура!"
И Новый Быт, даруя милость,
В тарелке держит осетра.
Варенье, ложечкой носимо,
Шипит и падает в боржом.
Жених, проворен нестерпимо,
К невесте лепится ужом.
И председатель на отвале,
Чете играя похвалу,
Приносит в выборгском бокале
Вино солдатское, халву,
И, принимая красный спич,
Сидит на столике кулич.

"Ура! Ура!" – поют заводы,
Картошкой дым под небеса.
И вот супруги, выпив соды,
Сидят и чешут волоса.
И стало все благоприятно:
Явилась ночь, ушла обратно,
И за окошком через миг
Погасла свечка-пятерик.

    1927

ДВИЖЕНИЕ

Сидит извозчик как на троне,
Из ваты сделана броня,
И борода, как на иконе,

But now the guests are gathering,
The steelworks chant "Hurray! Hurray!"
The New Life, a benevolent king,
Brings royal sturgeon on a tray.
Candied fruit passed around the room
Sizzles and drowns in soda water.
Insufferable sneak, the groom
Clings to the bride, and twirls about her.
The wedding chairman, full and smug,
Sings praise to the enchanting pair,
Brings soldier's wine, a crystal jug
From Vyborg, and halvah, and there
Upon a table a kulich
Listens to the Bolshevik's speech.

"Hurray! Hurray!" – the plants sing up,
Potato smoke-puffs soar up high.
The couple drink a soda pop,
Comb their hair sitting eye to eye.
And things have settled in all parts:
The night arrives, the night departs,
A fifther candle* dies away
Behind the window, for the day.

   1927

MOTION

The driver sits as in an icon,
The coach box thrones his stately loins,
His cotton armour holds the lichen

---

* A candle weighing a fifth of a pound.

41

Лежит, монетами звеня.
А бедный конь руками машет,
То вытянется, как налим,
То снова восемь ног сверкают
В его блестящем животе.

1927

НА РЫНКЕ

В уборе из цветов и крынок
Открыл ворота старый рынок.

Здесь бабы толсты, словно кадки,
Их шаль невиданной красы,
И огурцы, как великаны,
Прилежно плавают в воде.
Сверкают саблями селедки,
Их глазки маленькие кротки,
Но вот, разрезаны ножом,
Они свиваются ужом.
И мясо, властью топора,
Лежит, как красная дыра,
И колбаса кишкой кровавой
В жаровне плавает корявой,
И вслед за ней кудрявый пес
Несет на воздух постный нос,
И пасть открыта, словно дверь,
И голова, как блюдо,
И ноги точные идут,
Сгибаясь медленно посередине.
Но что это? Он с видом сожаленья
Остановился наугад,

Of his stiff beard jingling with coins.
Meanwhile his poor horse flaps its arms,
Now strains and stretches like a burbot,
Now once again its eight legs flicker
Around its shiny abdomen.

   1927

AT THE MARKET

The market opens in the morning,
Clay jugs and flowers at every corner.

Here tradeswomen are big as barrels
In their breathtakingly fine shawls,
And pickled cucumbers, like giants,
Obediently bathe in brine.
Sabre-like herrings gleam white flame,
Their little eyes are meek and tame,
But now, cut up by sharpened steel,
They coil and curl up tight like eels.
Meat hangs, ruled by the butcher's ax,
A gaping hole, red on the racks,
And sausages, like bloody bowels,
Hiss on the grill full of hot coals.
A curly-coated mutt, up close,
Carries towards them its lenten nose,
Its jaws hang open like a gate,
Its head a serving platter,
And its precise legs go along
Flexing deliberately in the middle.
But what is that? With a repentant look
It stops uncertain, shifts sidewise,

И слезы, точно виноград,
Из глаз по воздуху летят.

Калеки выстроились в ряд.
Один играет на гитаре.
Ноги обрубок, брат утрат,
Его кормилец на базаре.
А на обрубке том костыль,
Как деревянная бутыль.

Росток руки другой нам кажет,
Он ею хвастается, машет,
Он палец вывихнул, урод,
И визгнул палец, словно крот,
И хрустнул кости перекресток,
И сдвинулось лицо в наперсток.

А третий, закрутив усы,
Глядит воинственным героем.
Над ним в базарные часы
Мясные мухи вьются роем.
Он в банке едет на колесах,
Во рту запрятан крепкий руль,
В могилке где-то руки сохнут,
В какой-то речке ноги спят.
На долю этому герою
Осталось брюхо с головою
Да рот, большой, как рукоять,
Рулем веселым управлять.

Вон бабка с неподвижным оком
Сидит на стуле одиноком,
И книжка в дырочках волшебных
(Для пальцев милая сестра)
Поет чиновников служебных,
И бабка пальцами быстра.

And grape-like tears drop from its eyes
To float on air up to the sky.

Three cripples lined up in a row.
One strums the strings of his guitar.
A stump-leg certifies his woes,
And earns his bread at the bazaar.
And on his stump sits an embattled
Peg in the shape of a wooden bottle.

Another one shows off a sprout
That is his arm, waves it about.
He twists his thumb up like a screw,
The freakish thumb shrieks like a shrew,
A criss-cross bone cracks up and buckles,
His thimble of a face all puckers.

The third one twirls his big moustache,
He looks a hero, brave and brash.
At market hours, all over him
Flesh flies swirl buzzing in a swarm.
He drives a tin can set on wheels,
A handle firm between his teeth,
Arms wither somewhere in a grave,
Legs slumber somewhere in a river.
This hero kept for spoils of war
His head, his paunch and little more,
And kept his mouth, wide as a scar,
To turn the jolly handlebar.

An old hag with a frozen stare,
Sits each day on a lonely chair.
Her book, a sweetheart to the finger,
With magic bumps on pages spilled
Sings office clerks and thereby brings her
Much-needed comfort through her skill.

А вкруг – весы, как магелланы,
Отрепья масла, жир любви,
Уроды, словно истуканы,
В густой расчетливой крови,
И визг молитвенной гитары,
И шапки полны, как тиары,
Блестящей медью. Недалек
Тот миг, когда в норе опасной
Он и она – он пьяный, красный
От стужи, пенья и вина,
Безрукий, пухлый, и она –
Слепая ведьма – спляшут мило
Прекрасный танец-козерог,
Да так, что затрещат стропила
И брызнут искры из-под ног!

И лампа взвоет, как сурок.

    1927

ИВАНОВЫ

Стоят чиновные деревья,
Почти влезая в каждый дом.
Давно их кончено кочевье,
Они в решетках, под замком.
Шумит бульваров теснота,
Домами плотно заперта.

Но вот все двери растворились,
Повсюду шепот пробежал:
На службу вышли Ивановы
В своих штанах и башмаках.

Shop scales, Magellans, swirl around,
Tatters of butter, schmaltz of lust,
Unsightly idols, wounds unbound
With thickly calculated crusts;
Mid the guitar's shrill evocations
Hats, like tiaras, hold donations
Of shiny copper. Now night calls,
And shortly to a shady lair
They will return, a lovely pair:
He, – armless, round, flushed from the cold,
Liquor and song, – and she, an old
Blind witch – they'll dance the capricorn,
The ever-cheerful dance of fools,
With floor beams groaning, laces torn
And bright sparks flying from their soles!

And the oil lamp screeching like a mole.

   1927

THE IVANOVS

The office-dweller trees stand still
Pressing against the city blocks.
They roam no more, they've lost their will
Behind the bars, under the locks.
The tightness of the boulevards hums
Between the stifling rows of homes.

But now the doors are all thrown open,
The rumour runs along the streets:
The Ivanovs go to the office,
Shoes shined and baggy trousers pressed.

Пустые гладкие трамваи
Им подают свои скамейки.
Герои входят, покупают
Билетов хрупкие дощечки,
Сидят и держат их перед собой,
Не увлекаясь быстрою ездой.

А там, где каменные стены,
И рев гудков, и шум колес,
Стоят волшебные сирены
В клубках оранжевых волос.
Иные, дуньками одеты,
Сидеть не могут взаперти.
Прищелкивая в кастаньеты,
Они идут. Куда идти,
Кому нести кровавый ротик,
У чьей постели бросить ботик
И дернуть кнопку на груди?
Неужто некуда идти?

О мир, свинцовый идол мой,
Хлещи широкими волнами
И этих девок упокой
На перекрестке вверх ногами!
Он спит сегодня, грозный мир:
В домах спокойствие и мир.

Ужели там найти мне место,
Где ждет меня моя невеста,
Где стулья выстроились в ряд,
Где горка – словно Арарат –
Имеет вид отменно важный,
Где стол стоит и трехэтажный
В железных латах самовар
Шумит домашним генералом?

The sleek and empty streetcars offer
The Ivanovs their lacquered seats.
The heroes enter, pay the fare,
Obtain the tickets, flimsy slats,
Sit down and hold them stiffly to the side,
Impervious to the thrill of a speedy ride.

And where wheels roll and car horns wail
Among the brick and stone walls, there
Stand sirens from a fairy tale
With their frayed skeins of orange hair.
Some of them, dressed matryoshka-like,
Are bored indoors, loathe to lie low.
They're on the go, they stride and strike
Their castanets. But where to go?
Where would they carry their blood-red
Kissable lips, by whose day-bed
They'd shed a shoe and tug a bow?
Isn't there anywhere to go?

O world, my leaden idol, crest
High with broad waves, lash out and pound
The coast, and let these lasses rest
Here at the crossroads, upside down!
Today the wrathful world sleeps tight:
In all the homes there's peace and quiet.

But is my destiny a room
Where there's a bride and I'm the groom,
Where chairs are lined up by the wall,
A mountain of a cupboard, tall
As Ararat, looms pompously,
Where on the table puffs a three-
Floor samovar in iron armour,
The household general-in-chief?

О мир, свернись одним кварталом,
Одной разбитой мостовой,
Одним проплеванным амбаром,
Одной мышиною норой,
Но будь к оружию готов:
Целует девку – Иванов!

1928

СВАДЬБА

Сквозь окна хлещет длинный луч,
Могучий дом стоит во мраке.
Огонь раскинулся, горюч,
Сверкая в каменной рубахе.
Из кухни пышет дивным жаром.
Как золотые битюги,
Сегодня зреют там недаром
Ковриги, бабы, пироги.
Там кулебяка из кокетства
Сияет сердцем бытия.
Над нею проклинает детство
Цыпленок, синий от мытья.
Он глазки детские закрыл,
Наморщил разноцветный лобик
И тельце сонное сложил
В фаянсовый столовый гробик.
Над ним не поп ревел обедню,
Махая по ветру крестом,
Ему кукушка не певала
Коварной песенки своей:
Он был закован в звон капусты,
Он был томатами одет,

Curl up, my world, onto yourself,
Shrink to one block with broken pavement,
One spit-bespattered barn for life,
One dimly lit mousehole apartment,
But plan for war, do not relax:
An Ivanov kisses a lass!

1928

A WEDDING

Long beams of light gush through the walls,
The house stands in the dark alone,
The headstrong fire blazes and sprawls
And sends sparks from its robe of stone;
The kitchen gives out delightful heat.
Today, like golden thoroughbreds,
There ripen, for a reason, sweet
Pies, babkas, loaves and gingerbreads.
There, at the heart of all existence,
A showy fish pie takes the stage.
Above, a blue-washed chicken glistens
Cursing its innocent young age.
Its tight-shut childlike eyes are tame,
Its wrinkled brow piebald and roughened,
It tucks its drowsy little frame
Into a tabletop porcelain coffin.
No priest roared over it a mass
Waving a big cross to the wind,
No cuckoo ever sang for it
Her treacherous, deceitful rhyme:
But it was chained with cabbage clang,
And dressed all over with tomatoes,

Над ним, как крестик, опускался
На тонкой ножке сельдерей.
Так он почил в расцвете дней,
Ничтожный карлик средь людей.

Часы гремят. Настала ночь.
В столовой пир горяч и пылок.
Графину винному невмочь
Расправить огненный затылок.
Мясистых баб большая стая
Сидит вокруг, пером блистая,
И лысый венчик горностая
Венчает груди, ожирев
В поту столетних королев.
Они едят густые сласти,
Хрипят в неутоленной страсти
И распуская животы,
В тарелки жмутся и цветы.
Прямые лысые мужья
Сидят, как выстрел из ружья,
Едва вытягивая шеи
Сквозь мяса жирные траншеи.
И пробиваясь сквозь хрусталь
Многообразно однозвучный,
Как сон земли благополучной,
Парит на крылышках мораль.

О пташка божья, где твой стыд?
И что к твоей прибавит чести
Жених, приделанный к невесте
И позабывший звон копыт?
Его лицо передвижное
Еще хранит следы венца,
Кольцо на пальце золотое
Сверкает с видом удальца,
И поп, свидетель всех ночей,

Upon it, like a tiny cross
They hung a slender stalk of thyme.
Thus it expired still in its prime,
A wretched dwarf among mankind.

The wall clock booms. The night arrives.
The dinner rolls, a burning gyre.
A crystal vodka carafe strives
To flex its neck shot through with fire.
A bulging flock of fleshy dames
Sit round; their feathers are like flames,
A balding ermine crown that frames
Their ample bosoms dimly sheens
In the sweat of centenarian queens.
Their breath coarse with unsated passions,
They munch on glutinous confections,
They let their guts loose from the laces,
And press close to the plates and vases.
Their husbands, bald-headed and stifled,
Sit straight as the firing of a rifle,
They stretch their necks, but fail to stick
Out of the meat ruts, rich and thick.
And breaking through the crystal ring,
Monotonously polyphonic, –
Morality, the earth's hedonic
Dream, hovers on its flimsy wing.

Where is your shame, heavenly bird?
What do you gain, what worth or pride,
When a groom affixed to a bride
Forgets the feel of a horse well spurred?
His movable and fluid face
Still keeps the trace of a wedding wreath,
His golden ring, like saving grace,
Glares on his finger looking blithe.
The priest, a witness of the night,

Раскинув бороду забралом,
Сидит, как башня, перед балом
С большой гитарой на плече.

Так бей, гитара! Шире круг!
Ревут бокалы пудовые.
И вздрогнул поп, завыл и вдруг
Ударил в струны золотые.
И под железный гром гитары
Подняв последний свой бокал,
Несутся бешеные пары
В нагие пропасти зеркал.
И вслед за ними по засадам,
Ополоумев от вытья,
Огромный дом, виляя задом,
Летит в пространство бытия.
А там – молчанья грозный сон,
Седые полчища заводов,
И над становьями народов –
Труда и творчества закон.

1928

84 / ФОКСТРОТ

В ботинках кожи голубой,
В носках блистательного франта,
Парит по воздуху герой
В дыму гавайского джаз-банда.
Внизу – бокалов воркотня,
Внизу – ни ночи нет, ни дня,
Внизу – на выступе оркестра,
Как жрец, качается маэстро.
Он бьет рукой по животу,

Sits towering on the ballroom riser,
His beard unfurled like a knight's visor,
A huge guitar tucked by his side.

Let the guitar ring on! Make room!
The hogshead glasses bang and bounce.
The priest howls out, shudders and – boom! –
Strikes at the golden strings at once.
By the guitar's metallic clangours,
With one gulp having quenched their thirst,
Into the stark abyss of mirrors
Furious couples rush head first.
And after them, out of its mind
From ruckus, as in a hurdle race
The massive house wobbles its behind
Hurtling through existential space.
There's silence in its solemn slumber,
And factories in hoary smoke,
And over the tents of human folk
The law supreme of art and labour.

   1928

FOXTROT

His sky-blue shoes are all pizzazz,
His socks befit a dazzling dandy:
In cloud-puffs of Hawaiian jazz
The hero hovers like a candy.
Below the glasses coo away,
Below it's neither night, nor day,
Below, as in a priestly trance,
The maestro does his pagan dance.
He flaps his arms about, to stick

Он машет палкой в пустоту,
И легких галстуков извилина
На грудь картонную пришпилена.

Ура! Ура! Герой парит –
Гавайский фокус над Невою!
А бал ревет, а бал гремит,
Качая бледною толпою.
А бал гремит, единорог,
И бабы выставили в пляске
У перекрестка гладких ног
Чижа на розовой подвязке.
Смеется чиж – гляди, гляди!
Но бабы дальше ускакали,
И медным лесом впереди
Гудит фокстрот на пьедестале.

И так играя, человек
Родил в последнюю минуту
Прекраснейшего из калек –
Женоподобного Иуду.
Не тронь его и не буди,
не пригодится он для дела –
С цыплячьим знаком на груди
Росток болезненного тела.
А там, над бедною землей,
Во славу винам и кларнетам
Парит по воздуху герой,
Стреляя в небо пистолетом.

1928

Into the void his pointed stick,
The frills of his cravat meander
Along his chest in cardboard splendour.

Hourray! Hourray! The hero soars –
Behold, Neva, Hawaiian charm!
Meanwhile, the dance rumbles and roars
And swings the pale crowd in its storm.
The dance roars on, a unicorn,
And matrons show off ever smarter
The crossroads of smooth legs, adorned
With a siskin on a rosy garter.
Look on, look on! – the siskin laughs,
The matrons, though, have skipped away;
And still the foxtrot booms and puffs,
A brazen forest in the bay.

Thus, playing on till closing time
For the delight of multitudes
Man bore a child, the most sublime
Of cripples, an effeminate Judas.
Do not disturb him, let him rest
He is not fit for worthwhile labour –
With hatchling sign across his chest,
A sickly seedling, weak and sombre.
But up above these wretched shores
A god of tunes, a wine apostle,
Up in the air the hero soars
And shoots the sky out of his pistol!

   1928

57

ПЕКАРНЯ

В волшебном царстве калачей,
Где дым струится над пекарней,
Железный крендель, друг ночей,
Светил небесных светозарней.
Внизу под кренделем – содом.
Там тесто, выскочив из квашен,
Встает подобьем белых башен
И рвется в битву напролом.

Вперед! Настало время боя!
Ломая тысячи преград,
Оно ползет, урча и воя,
И не желает лезть назад.
Трещат столы, трясутся стены,
С высоких балок льет вода.
Но вот, подняв фонарь военный,
В чугун ударил тамада, –
И хлебопеки сквозь туман,
Как будто идолы в тиарах,
Летят, играя на цимбалах
Кастрюль неведомый канкан.

Как изукрашенные стяги,
Лопаты ходят тяжело,
И теста ровные корчаги
Плывут в квадратное жерло.
И в этой, красной от натуги,
Пещере всех метаморфоз
Младенец-хлеб приподнял руки
И слово стройно произнес.

THE BAKERY

There in the magic land of loaves,
Where smoke swirls from the bakery,
More glorious than the starry droves,
An iron pretzel holds its see.
Beneath the pretzel is an uproar:
The dough has leapt out of the troughs.
It towers like chalk-white seaside cliffs
And bursts into an all-out war.

Advance! The time is ripe for battles!
Reducing barriers to a wreck,
It clambers forth, it growls and rattles,
Not going to be kneaded back.
The tables creak, the walls are crumbling,
Water spurts from the ceiling beams.
But the emcee strikes on the rumbling
Cast iron, his war lantern gleams,
And bakers fly with their tall hats
Cleaving the mist like ancient idols
In crowns; they hammer on their cymbals
An eerie cancan of the pots.

The burdened peels, like festive flags,
Heavily shuttle to and fro,
The crater swallows the dough slugs
Ranged orderly row after row.
And in this grotto red with strain,
This seat of metamorphosis,
The baby bread puts forth its plain,
Harmonious word, hands raised in bliss.

И пекарь огненной трубой
Трубил о нем во мрак ночной.

А печь, наследника родив
И стройное поправив чрево,
Стоит стыдливая, как дева
С ночною розой на груди.
И кот, в почетном сидя месте,
Усталой лапкой рыльце крестит,
Зловонным хвостиком вертит,
Потом кувшинчиком сидит.
Сидит, сидит, и улыбнется,
И вдруг исчез. Одно болотце
Осталось в глиняном полу.
И утро выплыло в углу.

1928

РЫБНАЯ ЛАВКА

И вот, забыв людей коварство,
Вступаем мы в иное царство.
Тут тело розовой севрюги,
Прекраснейшей из всех севрюг,
Висело, вытянувши руки,
Хвостом прикреплено на крюк.
Под ней кета пылала мясом,
Угри, подобные колбасам,
В копченой пышности и лени
Дымились, подогнув колени,
И среди них, как желтый клык,
Сиял на блюде царь-балык.
О самодержец пышный брюха,

The baker blows his fiery horn
Announcing to the night: it's born.

The mother oven takes a rest,
Her shapely belly now unladen,
She's a demure and modest maiden,
A rose nocturnal on her breast.
A cat takes the presiding place,
And sits there like an earthen vase,
Its paw crosses its whiskered snout,
Malodorous tail twirls about.
And so it sits. It sits and sneers,
Then suddenly it disappears,
Only a muddy pool stays on.
Slowly, the room wells up with dawn.

   1928

AT THE FISHMONGER'S

Now, leave behind the guile of man:
We come into a different land.
There, the body of a rosy sturgeon,
The most delightful of them all,
Arms dangling, blushing like a virgin,
Hung from the hook along the wall.
The flesh of salmon flashed below;
Sausage-like eels, laid in a row
With knees tucked in, languid and tender,
Gave out the fumes of smoky splendour,
Amid them, like a yellowed tusk,
Balyk the tsar glowed in the dusk.
O glorious lord of the intestine!

Кишечный бог и властелин,
Руководитель тайный духа
И помыслов архитриклин!
Хочу тебя! Отдайся мне!
Дай жрать тебя до самой глотки!
Мой рот трепещет, весь в огне,
Кишки дрожат, как готтентотки.
Желудок, в страсти напряжен,
Голодный сок струями точит,
То вытянется, как дракон,
То вновь сожмется что есть мочи,
Слюна, клубясь, во рту бормочет,
И сжаты челюсти вдвойне…
Хочу тебя! Отдайся мне!
Повсюду гром консервных банок,
Ревут сиги, вскочив в ушат.
Ножи, торчащие из ранок,
Качаются и дребезжат.
Горит садок подводным светом,
Где за стеклянною стеной
Плывут лещи, объяты бредом,
Галлюцинацией, тоской,
Сомненьем, ревностью, тревогой…
И смерть над ними, как торгаш,
Поводит бронзовой острогой.
Весы читают "Отче наш",
Две гирьки, мирно встав на блюдце,
Определяют жизни ход,
И дверь звенит, и рыбы бьются,
И жабры дышат наоборот.

1928

O gastric god, one of a kind,
The spirit's master, most clandestine!
You, architriclinus of mind!
I want you! Give yourself to me!
How I devoured you in my thoughts!
My palate burns incessantly,
My guts shiver like Hottentots.
My stomach swells with passion, boils
Exuding streams of hungry nectar;
Now, dragon-like, it tightly coils,
Now shrinks and sags, a feeble splatter;
My mouth is filled with spit and sputter,
Jaws clenched with savage energy…
I want you! Give yourself to me!
There's tin can ruckus everywhere,
Whitefish jump roaring into vats,
And carving knives tremble in the air
Sticking out of neat little cuts.
Behind the glass of the aquarium,
In the green glow of man-made sea
The dreamy breams float in delirium,
Hallucinations and ennui,
Full of resentment, doubt and fear…
And, looming over, like a huckster,
Death shakes at them his brazen spear.
The shop scale says the Paternoster,
Two little weights on a tin platter
Decide the life's mysterious course,
The fishes thrash, doors squeak and chatter,
And throbbing gills breathe in reverse.

   1928

ОБВОДНЫЙ КАНАЛ

В моем окне на весь квартал
Обводный царствует канал.

Ломовики, как падишахи,
Коня запутав медью блях,
Идут, закутаны в рубахи,
С нелепой важностью нерях.
Вокруг пивные встали в ряд,
Ломовики в пивных сидят.
И в окна конских морд толпа
Глядит, мотаясь у столба,
И в окна конских морд собор
Глядит, поставленный в упор.
А там за ним, за морд собором,
Течет толпа на полверсты,
Кричат слепцы блестящим хором,
Стальные вытянув персты.
Маклак штаны на воздух мечет,
Ладонью бьет, поет как кречет:
Маклак – владыка всех штанов,
Ему подвластен ход миров,
Ему подвластно толп движенье,
Толпу томит штанов круженье,
И вот – она, забывши честь,
Стоит, не в силах глаз отвесть,
Вся прелесть и изнеможенье.

Кричи, маклак, свисти уродом,
Мечи штаны под облака!
Но перед сомкнутым народом
Иная движется река:
Один – сапог несет на блюде,
Другой поет хвалу Иуде,

THE BYPASS CANAL

Outside my window, ruling all
The block, is the Bypass Canal.

Dray drivers walk like padishahs,
Their horses snarled in buckles and clamps,
In their long shirts, with their set jaws
And the silly pompousness of scamps.
Pubs stand around; in every pub
The drivers have their booze and grub.
And through the windows stares a host
Of horse heads swaying by the post,
And through the windows stares a flight
Of horse heads packed together tight.
And past the host of horses, crowds
Flood the embankment for a mile,
A dazzling choir of blind men shouts,
Extending fingers stiff as steel.
A hawker slaps his hand, unfurling
A pair of pants, he sings like merlin,
He is the sovereign of all pants,
He rules the motion of the planets,
He rules the currents of the crowd
Dazed by the whirling pants and awed;
The crowd stares on, it longs to see,
It has now lost all decency,
Delighted, languid and spellbound.

Yell, hawker, whistle like a freak,
And hurl your pants to heaven high!
But there before the gawking folk
Another river rushes by:
One holds a tray, on it two booties,
Another sings a hymn to Judas,

А третий, грозен и румян,
В кастрюлю бьет, как в барабан.
И нету сил держаться боле,
Толпа в плену, толпа в неволе,
Толпа лунатиком идет,
Ладони вытянув вперед.

А вкруг – черны заводов замки,
Высок под облаком гудок.
И вот опять идут мустанги
На колоннаде пышных ног.
И воют жалобно телеги,
И плещет взорванная грязь,
И над каналом спят калеки,
К пустым бутылкам прислонясь.

    1928

БРОДЯЧИЕ МУЗЫКАНТЫ

Закинув на спину трубу,
Как бремя золотое,
Он шел, в обиде на судьбу.
За ним бежали двое.
Один, сжимая скрипки тень,
Горбун и шаромыжка,
Скрипел и плакал каждый день,
Как потная подмышка.
Другой, искусник и борец,
И чемпион гитары,
Огромный нес в руках крестец

A third one, ruddy-cheeked and glum,
Beats on a pot as on a drum.
The crowd is stricken to the core,
The crowd can't bear it anymore,
Held captive by the magic charms,
They sleepwalk and stretch out their arms.

Works stand like castles casting shade,
Their lofty hoots soar to the sky,
And mustangs on the colonnade
Of their lush legs walk slowly by.
The horse-drawn wagons squeal and whimper,
Road dirt explodes and splashes wide,
And by the Channel cripples slumber
With empty bottles by their side.

   1928

VAGRANT MUSICIANS

He strode, resentful of his lot,
Behind his back a load
Of gold, a horn tied in a knot.
Two others briskly followed.
One clutched a fiddle's darkened shade,
He was a hunchbacked dimwit,
All day his bow creaked and complained
Like an ever-sweaty armpit.
The other one, a heavyweight
And a champ on the guitar,
Lugged a huge sacrum with the great

С роскошной песнею Тамары.
На том крестце семь струн железных,
И семь валов, и семь колков,
Рукой построены полезной,
Болтались в виде уголков.

На стогнах солнце опускалось,
Неслись извозчики гурьбой,
Как бы фигуры пошехонцев
На волокнистых лошадях.
И вдруг в колодце между окон
Возник трубы волшебный локон,
Он прянул вверх тупым жерлом
И заревел. Глухим орлом
Был первый звук. Он, грохнув, пал,
За ним второй орел предстал,
Орлы в кукушек превращались,
Кукушки в точки уменьшались,
И точки, горло сжав в комок,
Упали в окна всех домов.

Тогда горбатик, скрипочку
Приплюснув подбородком,
Слепил перстом улыбочку
На личике коротком,
И, визгнув поперечиной,
По маленьким струнам,
Заплакал, искалеченный:
– Тилим-там-там!

Система тронулась в порядке.
Качались знаки вымысла.

Song of the splendid Queen Tamar.*
And it had seven iron strings
And seven pins, and seven shafts,
Dangling like little angled things,
Made by a hand skilled in the craft.

The sun was setting on the broadways,
Street coaches rushed along in throngs
With stringy horses held in harness
And drivers poised like philistines.
And then, the magic curl and bell
Sprang up inside the windowed well.
The muzzle bellowed, its first sound
Was a deaf eagle. It hit the ground
And with a boom came to a close.
Another eagle then arose.
Eagles turned into cuckoo birds,
And cuckoos shrank to tiny curds,
They choked the throat and made their fall
Through all the windows in the wall.

The hunchback tucked the violin
Under his chin and moulded
On his misshapen face a grin
With a finger oddly folded.
He took his screechy bow and swung,
For wounded sounds to come
Out of his fiddle tightly strung:
– Tilim-tum-tum!

The system then set off in order.
Tokens of fancy quavered.

* A popular song, a Lermontov poem set to music. The lines "And all
through the night one could hear // A fervent and passionate hum" are a
direct quotation from the poem.

69

И каждый слушатель украдкой
Слезою чистой вымылся,
Когда на подоконниках
Средь музыки и грохота
Легла толпа поклонников
В подштанниках и кофтах.

Но богослов житейской страсти
И чемпион гитары
Подъял крестец, поправил части
И с песней нежною Тамары
Уста отважно растворил.
И все умолкло.
Звук самодержавный,
Глухой, как шум Куры,
Роскошный, как мечта,
Пронесся…
И в этой песне сделалась видна
Тамара на кавказском ложе.
Пред нею, полные вина,
Шипели кубки дотемна
И юноши стояли тоже.
И юноши стояли,
Махали руками,
И страстные дикие звуки
Всю ночь раздавалися там…
– Тилим-там-там!

Певец был строен и суров.
Он пел, трудясь, среди дворов
Средь выгребных высоких ям
Трудился он, могуч и прям.
Вокруг него система кошек,
Система окон, ведер, дров
Висела, темный мир размножив
На царства узкие дворов.

And all who listened were rewarded
With clear tears, shy and wayward,
When eager gents and damsels
In cardigans and underpants
Propped up their heads on windowsills
To the din and thunder of the band.

But then the sage of worldly passions
And champ on the guitar
Held up the sacrum, finely fashioned,
And with the sweet song of Tamar
He parted valiantly his lips.
And all fell silent.
And the sovereign sound,
Muffled like the Kura's rumble,
Resplendent like a dream
Swept over…
And in this song Tamar came into sight,
On her Caucasian couch reclined.
Beside her, goblets full of bright
Wine, sparkled well into the night
And young lads also stood around.
Lads stood around
And waved their arms,
And all through the night one could hear
A fervent and passionate hum…
– Tilim-tum-tum!

The singer, who was stern and strong,
Toiled in the courtyard on his song;
By an exalted dumpster pit
He laboured, full of grace and grit.
Round him a system of stray cats,
A system of pails, firewood, windows
Hung in the darkening world and cut
It into thin prismatic kingdoms.

Но что был двор? Он был трубою,
Он был тоннелем в те края,
Где был и я гоним судьбою,
Где пропадала жизнь моя.
Где сквозь мансардное окошко
При лунном свете, вся дрожа,
В глаза мои смотрела кошка,
Как дух седьмого этажа.

1928

НА ЛЕСТНИЦАХ

Коты на лестницах упругих,
Большие рыла приподняв,
Сидят, как будды, на перилах,
Ревут, как трубы, о любви.
Нагие кошечки, стесняясь,
Друг к дружке жмутся, извиняясь.
Кокетки! Сколько их кругом!
Они по кругу ходят боком,
Они текут любовным соком,
Они трясутся, на весь дом
Распространяя запах страсти.
Коты ревут, открывши пасти,-
Они как дьяволы вверху
В своем серебряном меху.

Один лишь кот в глухой чужбине
Сидит, задумчив, не поет.
В его взъерошенной овчине
Справляют блохи хоровод.
Отшельник лестницы печальной,

What was this courtyard, but a chimney?
A tunnel to a distant land,
Where the heart was withering within me,
Where fate had me exiled and banned.
Where through the attic window, by
The moonlight, trembling to the core,
A stray cat looked me in the eye,
A spirit of the seventh floor.

   1928

ON THE STAIRS

On springy urban stairways, tomcats
Sit with their stocky muzzles up,
They perch like Buddhas on the railings,
Bugling, like trumpets, of their love.
Nude pussycats, coy and befuddled,
Apologetically cuddle
Together. Oh, coquettes! Unfussed,
They sidle to the cats, they move,
In circles, ooze the sap of love,
They tremble, sending whiffs of lust
Along the steps to every floor.
The tomcats open their maws and roar,
They look like devils up the stairs
With their thick coats of silver hair.

But there's one, lonesome and remote,
Who's lost in thought, who does not sing.
In his dishevelled sheepskin coat
Lighthearted fleas go frolicking.
A monk of shadowy staircases,

Монах помойного ведра,
Он мир любви первоначальной
Напрасно ищет до утра.
Сквозь дверь он чувствует квартиру,
Где труд дневной едва лишь начат.
Там от плиты и до сортира
Лишь бабьи туловища скачут.
Там примус выстроен, как дыба,
На нем, от ужаса треща,
Чахоточная воет рыба
В зеленых масляных прыщах.
Там трупы вымытых животных
Лежат на противнях холодных
И чугуны, купели слез,
Венчают зла апофеоз.

Кот поднимается, трепещет.
Сомненья нету: замкнут мир
И лишь одни помои плещут
Туда, где мудрости кумир.
И кот встает на две ноги,
Идет вперед, подъемля лапы.
Пропала лестница. Ни зги
В глазах. Шарахаются бабы,
Но поздно! Кот, на шею сев,
Как дьявол, бьется, озверев,
Рвет тело, жилы отворяет,
Когтями кости вынимает…
О, боже, боже, как нелеп!
Сбесился он или ослеп?

Шла ночь без горечи и страха,
И любопытным виден был
Семейный сад – кошачья плаха,
Где месяц медленный всходил.
Деревья дружные качали

A hermit of the garbage pail,
All through the night till dawn he traces
Primeval love – to no avail.
He senses an apartment through
The door. The daily toil commences.
Between the kitchen and the loo
Prance busy female corpulences.
On a gas stove built like a rack,
A terrified fish wails and sputters
And wastes away, sprawled on its back,
All covered in green oily blisters.
On chilly baking sheets there rest
Animal corpses, washed and dressed.
A font of tears, the pot for sauces
Completes the evil apotheosis.

The cat stands up, shudders and stops.
No doubt: the world is sealed around,
And nothing splashes there but slops,
Where roams the sage, by wisdom crowned.
The cat rears up and claws the air,
He lumbers forth on his two feet.
It is pitch dark. There's no more stairs
In sight. The stunned housewives retreat –
Too late! The devil is astride
Their necks. Possessed, he tears aside
The body, in mad fury draws
Their blood, pulls bones out with his claws…
Good Lord, is he absurd! What kind
Of crank is he? Has he gone blind?

The night carried no fear or spite,
And passersby saw in the yard
A cat-sized scaffold in the bright
Light of the moon, slow and unmarred.
The trees, with their big bodies blurred,

Большими сжатыми телами,
Нагие птицы верещали,
Скача неверными ногами.
Над ними, желтый скаля зуб,
Висел кота холодный труп.

Монах! Ты висельником стал!
Прощай. В моем окошке,
Справляя дикий карнавал,
Опять несутся кошки.
И я на лестнице стою,
Такой же белый, важный.
Я продолжаю жизнь твою,
Мой праведник отважный.

    1928

НЕЗРЕЛОСТЬ

Младенец кашку составляет
Из манных зерен голубых.
Зерно, как кубик, вылетает
Из легких пальчиков двойных.
Зерно к зерну – горшок наполнен,
И вот, качаясь, он висит,
Как колокол на колокольне,
Квадратной силой знаменит.
Ребенок лезет вдоль по чащам,
Ореховые рвет листы,
И над деревьями все чаще
его колеблются персты.
И девочки, носимы вместе,
К нему по облаку плывут.

Kept swaying to a common beat,
While naked birds endlessly chirred
And hopped on their uncertain feet.
The cat's cold corpse above them hung
Baring in a grin his yellow fang.

Monk, on the gallows you found your rest!
Farewell. My window shows
The cats, again in their wild fest,
Rushing through highs and lows.
Like you did, on the stairs I stand,
A man of heft and merit.
Your fire goes on, within me fanned,
Oh brave and righteous spirit!

   1928

IMMATURITY

An infant builds a porridge out
Of tiny bluish grains of wheat.
His twofold fingers nimbly route,
Like letter blocks, grains to their seat.
Thus, crumb by crumb, he fills the pot,
Hung like a bell on a bell tower
And slowly swinging; it is hot
And rings with its rectangular power.
Along the woods the infant clambers
And plucks the leaves from hazel trees,
His open palm sticks out and trembles
Above the treetops in the breeze.
Girls waft towards him, a cloud-borne flock,
And one of them takes off her cross,

Одна из них, снимая крестик,
Тихонько падает в траву.

Горшок клубится под ногою,
Огня субстанция жива,
И девочка лежит нагою,
В огонь откинув кружева.
Ребенок тихо отвечает:
"Младенец я и не окреп!
Ужель твой ум не примечает,
Насколь твой замысел нелеп?
Красот твоих мне стыден вид,
Закрой же ножки белой тканью,
Смотри, как мой костер горит,
И не готовься к поруганью!"
И, тихо взяв мешалку в руки,
Он мудро кашу помешал –
Так он урок живой науки
Душе несчастной преподал.

1928

НАРОДНЫЙ ДОМ

Народный Дом, курятник радости,
Амбар волшебного житья,
Корыто праздничное страсти,
Густое пекло бытия!
Тут шишаки красноармейские,
А с ними дамочки житейские
Неслись задумчивым ручьем.
Им шум столичный нипочем!
Тут радость пальчиком водила,

A little pendant from her neck,
And falls down quietly on the grass.

The pot swells, burbling underfoot
On the live body of the blaze;
The girl reposes in the nude
While flames consume her cast-off lace.
"I'm still a child, I'm not matured,"
The infant's quiet voice demurred,
"How can your mind be so assured,
When your design is so absurd?
To see your beauties I'm ashamed,
So cover your appearance
With a white cloth, observe my flame
And don't anticipate offence!"
He took a paddle and a bowl
And wisely gave his meal a stir,
And thus he taught the wretched soul
A lesson drawn from living lore.

　　1928

THE PEOPLE'S HOUSE

The People's House, a coop of joy,
A barn of otherworldly living,
A festive trough of energy,
A densely churning forge of being!
That's where Red Army pointed helmets
In tow with everyday coquettes
Flow like a pensive forest stream,
At home in the big city realm;
Joy drew its easy finger here

Она к народу шла потехою.
Тут каждый мальчик забавлялся:
Кто дамочку кормил орехами,
А кто над пивом забывался.
Тут гор американские хребты!
Над ними девочки, богини красоты,
В повозки быстрые запрятались.
Повозки катятся вперед,
Красотки нежные расплакались,
Упав совсем на кавалеров…
И много было тут других примеров.

Тут девка водит на аркане
Свою пречистую собачку,
Сама вспотела вся до нитки
И грудки выехали вверх.
А та собачка пречестная,
Весенним соком налитая,
Грибными ножками неловко
Вдоль по дорожке шелестит.

Подходит к девке именитой
Мужик роскошный, апельсинщик.
Он держит тазик разноцветный,
В нем апельсины аккуратные лежат.
Как будто циркулем очерченные круги,
Они волнисты и упруги;
Как будто маленькие солнышки, они
Легко катаются по жести
И пальчикам лепечут: "Лезьте, лезьте!"

И девка, кушая плоды,
Благодарит рублем прохожего.
Она зовет его на "ты",
Но ей другого хочется, хорошего.

And people are easy to amuse.
Here every lad is full of cheer:
He treats his lass to nuts and schmoozes,
Or muses on a mug of beer.
Here rollercoaster mountains loom above!
And on them pretty girls, like goddesses of love,
Are snugly tucked in speedy carriages
That roll along on shiny rails.
The gentle beauties burst in tears
And fall on their respective gents…
And there were many other such developments.

A lass is strolling with a lasso
Walking her venerable doggie,
Herself all sweaty to the bone,
Breasts nearly sliding up and out.
Meanwhile the honourable doggie
Full to the brim with April juices
Clumsily rustles on the pavement
With its mushroomy little feet.

A splendid chap, an orange-seller,
Comes to the notable young lady
And holds a brightly painted bucket
With oranges neatly arranged in even rows.
They are elastic, sinuous, they sparkle
Like perfect compass-drafted circles,
Like little yellow suns
They softly roll inside the tin
And murmur to the fingers, "Dive right in!"

The lass goes feasting on the fruit,
Her eyes fall on a passerby
As if she blessed him with a gift,
But she desires another, nicer guy.

Она хорошего глазами ищет,
Но перед ней качели свищут.

В качелях девочка-душа
Висела, ножкою шурша.
Она по воздуху летела
И теплой ножкою вертела,
И теплой ручкою звала.

Другой же, видя преломленное
Свое лицо в горбатом зеркале,
Стоял молодчиком оплеванным,
Хотел смеяться, но не мог.
Желая знать причину искривления,
Он как бы делался ребенком
И шел назад на четвереньках,
Под сорок лет – четвероног.

Но перед этим праздничным угаром
Иные будто спасовали:
Они довольны не амбаром радости,
Они тут в молодости побывали.
И вот теперь, шепча с бутылкою,
Прощаясь с молодостью пылкою,
Они скребут стакан зубами,
Они губой его высасывают,
Они приятелям рассказывают
Свои веселия шальные.
Ведь им бутылка словно матушка,
Души медовая салопница,
Целует слаще всякой девки,
А холодит сильнее Невки.

Они глядят в стекло.
В стекле восходит утро.
Фонарь, бескровный, как глиста,

She seeks the nice one with her wishing eyes
And sees the park swing swishing by.

A girl hung in there, sweet and cute,
Whispering with her dainty foot,
She flitted swiftly through the air
And twirled her warm foot with a flair
And beckoned with her sultry hand.

Meanwhile the other guy observing
His own face in a humpbacked mirror,
Stood stupefied, humiliated,
Couldn't find it in himself to laugh.
And looking for the cause of this contortion
He almost turned into a child
And clambered out on hands and knees:
A man of forty on all fours.

But some appear to shrink away
Before this frenzied festival:
A barn of joy would not content them,
Back in their youth they've seen it all.
Now, whispering with a bottle, they
Bid farewell to their youthful day:
They wrap their lips around the glass,
They gnaw on it and suck it out,
Recalling their outrageous antics
Before their friends who listen eagerly.
The bottle is their mother dear,
The honeyed scrounger of the soul,
Its kiss is sweeter than a lover's,
Its shiver colder than the river's.

They look out through the glass.
Behind the glass, dawn rises.
A streetlight joggles on its arm

Стрелой болтается в кустах.
И по трамваям рай качается –
Тут каждый мальчик улыбается,
А девочка наоборот –
Закрыв глаза, открыла рот
И ручку выбросила теплую
На приподнявшийся живот.

Трамвай, шатаясь, чуть идет.

1928

ЦИРК

Цирк сияет, словно щит,
Цирк на пальцах верещит,
Цирк на дудке завывает,
Душу в душу ударяет!
С нежным личиком испанки
И цветами в волосах
Тут девочка, пресветлый ангел,
Виясь, плясала вальс-казак.
Она среди густого пара
Стоит, как белая гагара,
То с гитарой у плеча
Реет, ноги волоча.
То вдруг присвистнет, одинокая,
Совьется маленьким ужом,
И вновь несется, нежно охая, –
Прелестный образ и почти что нагишом!
Но вот одежды беспокойство
Вкруг тела складками легло.
Хотя напрасно!

In bushes, bloodless like a worm.
And paradise on tramway rails
Sways in the cars where each boy smiles,
And contrary to that, each bonnie
Girl sits, her eyes closed, her lips slightly
Ajar, her little warm hand thrown
Onto her softly rising belly.

The tram rolls on, but only barely.

1928

THE CIRCUS

The circus glitters like a medal,
The circus is a finger rattle,
The circus tootles a nose harp
And bangs a heart against a heart!
Here a Spanish-looking maiden,
A flower in her sable curls,
Like the sweetest, brightest angel
Does the sinuous Cossack waltz.
Amid the billowing white clouds
She stands, a snowy polar grouse,
Then she soars, her foot unsteady,
Her guitar held at the ready,
Then suddenly she gives a whistle
And twirls and twists, a tiny snake,
And darts again, all sighs and rustle, –
A lovely image, and she's practically naked!
Suddenly the folds and agitation
Of fabric wrapped her as she spun.
But all in vain!

Членов нежное устройство
На всех впечатление произвело.

Толпа встает. Все дышат, как сапожники,
Во рту слюны навар кудрявый.
Иные, даже самые безбожники,
Полны таинственной отравой.
Другие же, суя табак в пустую трубку,
Облизываясь, мысленно целуют ту голубку,
Которая пред ними пролетела.
Пресветлая! Остаться не захотела!

Вой всюду в зале тут стоит,
Кромешным духом все полны.
Но музыка опять гремит,
И все опять удивлены.
Лошадь белая выходит,
Бледным личиком вертя,
И на ней при всем народе
Сидит полновесное дитя.
Вот, маша руками враз,
Дитя, смеясь, сидит анфас,
И вдруг, взмахнув ноги обмылком,
Дитя сидит к коню затылком.
А конь, как стражник, опустив
Высокий лоб с большим пером,
По кругу носится, спесив,
Поставив ноги под углом.

Тут опять всеобщее изумленье,
И похвала, и одобренье,
И, как зверек, кусает зависть
Тех, кто недавно улыбались
Иль равнодушными казались.

Her limbs' delightful disposition
Already made an impression on everyone.

The crowd is on their feet. They pant like cobblers,
Spit brewing in their mouths in skeins.
And many start to feel, though they are godless,
A mystic poison in their veins.
While others stuff their empty pipes with fresh tobacco
And in their minds kiss this turtledove that flew by like an echo
And smack their lips, but she has flown away.
Oh, angel bright! Why didn't she want to stay?

And they all make an awful din,
But over the hullabaloo,
The music rumbles once again
And everyone's surprised anew.
A white horse steps into the ring,
Twirls its pale physiognomy.
And on the horse a child is riding,
A full-grown child, for all to see.
Now she rides full face and grins,
Now her arm around her spins,
Now with a swing of a soap-bar leg
She flips around like a square peg.
The horse keeps down its high plumed brow.
It's haughtily and strongly built,
And like a sentry, it goes round
Holding its long legs at a tilt.

And everybody is once again amazed,
The artists get applause and praise,
But envy, like a tiny rat,
Gnaws those who were amused, or sat
Looking indifferent and flat.

Мальчишка, тихо хулиганя,
Подружке на ухо шептал:
"Какая тут сегодня баня!"
И девку нежно обнимал.
Она же, к этому привыкнув,
Сидела тихая, не пикнув.
Закон имея естества,
Она желала сватовства.

Но вот опять арена скачет,
Ход представленья снова начат.
Два тоненькие мужика
Стоят, сгибаясь, у шеста.
Один, ладони поднимая,
На воздух медленно ползет,
То красный шарик выпускает,
То вниз, нарядный, упадет
И товарищу на плечи
Тонкой ножкою встает.
Потом они, смеясь опасно,
Ползут наверх единогласно
И там, обнявшись наугад,
На толстом воздухе стоят.
Они дыханьем укрепляют
Двойного тела равновесье,
Но через миг опять летают,
Себя по воздуху развеся.
Тут опять, восторга полон,
Зал трясется, как кликуша,
И стучит ногами в пол он,
Не щадя чужие уши.
Один старик интеллигентный
Сказал, другому говоря:
"Этот праздник разноцветный
Посещаю я не зря.
Здесь нахожу я греческие игры,

A young lad gets a little naughty
And whispers in his girlfriend's ear:
"A steamy place here, ain't it, hottie?"
And snuggles up close to his dear.
She sits obedient and quiet,
Because she is accustomed to it.
Compliant to the natural law,
She can't resist the nuptial draw.

But now the ring gallops in force,
Performance runs its further course.
A shiny pole stands in the centre.
Two scrawny gents presently enter.
One slowly lifts his hands, and soon,
Unhurried, crawls up on the air.
Now he lets out a red balloon,
Now in his snazzy sparkling wear
He drops back down, his dainty foot
On the shoulder of his pair.
They, then, with a precarious laugh
Unanimously climb the staff
And in a nonchalant embrace
Stand on the broad air face to face.
They take a breath to resupply
Their balance, then again a quick
Movement – and they hang out to dry
Around the air their dual physique.
All the stands go wild once more,
Bursting out with frenzied cheers,
Feet are stomping on the floor,
Never mind the neighbour's ears.
A gentleman, all grey and cultured,
Says to another speaking thus:
"Not for naught this multicoloured
Feast is so illustrious.
Here I discover games of Ancient Greece

Красоток розовые икры,
Научных замечаю лошадей, –
Это не цирк, а прямо чародей!"
Другой, плешивый, как колено,
Сказал, что это несомненно.

На последний страшный номер
Вышла женщина-змея.
Она усердно ползала в соломе,
Ноги в кольца завия.
Проползав несколько минут,
Она совсем лишилась тела.
Кругом служители бегут:
– Где? Где?
Красотка улетела!
Тут пошел в народе ужас,
Все свои хватают шапки
И бросаются наружу,
Имея девок полные охапки.
"Воры! Воры!" – все кричали.
Но воры были невидимки:
Они в тот вечер угощали
Своих друзей на Ситном рынке.
Над ними небо было рыто
Веселой руганью двойной,
И жизнь трещала, как корыто,
Летая книзу головой.

1928

And pretty girls with rosy knees,
I notice scientific horses, –
I say, it is a wizard of a circus!"
The other one, bald as a trout,
Says so it is, without a doubt.

For the last and scary number
A snake-girl comes to show her charms
And in the straw industriously clamber
Making corkscrews of her legs and arms.
After a minute of this crawling
She went discorporate at last.
All the circus hands come bawling:
– Where is she?
But away she passed!
Everyone jumps from their seat,
They are scared out of their senses,
Hats in hands, out to the street
They rush with armfuls of their wives and misses.
"Thieves!" – they yelled, and panic sparked,
But the thieves were disembodied:
For that night at the Sitny Market
They passed a bottle with their buddies.
The sky above was shovelled rough
With merry cursing strung around,
And life flew over like a trough
Crackling and hanging upside down.

1928

II

СМЕШАННЫЕ СТОЛБЦЫ

В ЖИЛИЩАХ НАШИХ

В жилищах наших
Мы тут живем умно и некрасиво.
Справляя жизнь, рождаясь от людей,
Мы забываем о деревьях.

Они поистине металла тяжелей
В зеленом блеске сомкнутых кудрей.
Иные, кроны поднимая к небесам,
Как бы в короны спрятали глаза,
И детских рук изломанная прелесть,
Одетая в кисейные листы,
Еще плодов удобных не наелась
И держит звонкие плоды.

Так сквозь века, селенья и сады
Мерцают нам удобные плоды.
Нам непонятна эта красота –
Деревьев влажное дыханье.
Вон дровосеки, позабыв топор,
Стоят и смотрят, тихи, молчаливы.
Кто знает, что подумали они,
Что вспомнили и что открыли,
Зачем, прижав к холодному стволу
Свое лицо, неудержимо плачут?

Вот мы нашли поляну молодую,
Мы встали в разные углы,
Мы стали тоньше. Головы растут,

II

MIXED COLUMNS

HERE IN OUR DWELLINGS

Here in our dwellings
We live our beautiless and clever lives.
While tackling life, while being born of women,
We let the trees slip out of our minds.

They verily are heavier than iron,
Their crowded tresses are of brilliant green.
They stand with canopies uplifted to the skies,
As if under the crowns they hide their eyes.
Their childlike arms, a twisted loveliness,
Are not yet sated with the handy food
Of fruit, and decked out in the muslin dress
Of leaves, they bear the sonorous fruits.

Thus, through the orchards, settlements and ages
The handy fruits have always shimmered at us.
We cannot comprehend this beauty,
The dewy breathing of the trees.
Look: lumberjacks have put aside their axes,
They stand and gaze in silent resignation.
And who can tell what's going through their minds,
What they recall, what they discover,
And why, with faces firmly pressed against
The cool tree trunks, they cannot help but weep?

Here, we have found a young glade in the woods,
We stand in its opposing corners,
We're getting thinner, and our heads grow larger,

И небо приближается навстречу.
Затвердевают мягкие тела,
Блаженно дервенеют вены,
И ног проросших больше не поднять,
Не опустить раскинутые руки.
Глаза закрылись, времена отпали,
И солнце ласково коснулось головы.

В ногах проходят влажные валы.
Уж влага поднимается, струится
И омывает лиственные лица:
Земля ласкает детище свое.
А вдалеке над городом дымится
Густое фонарей копье.

Был город осликом, четырехстенным домом.
На двух колесах из камней
Он ехал в горизонте плотном,
Сухие трубы накреня.
Был светлый день. Пустые облака,
Как пузыри морщинистые, вылетали.
Шел ветер, огибая лес.
И мы стояли, тонкие деревья,
В бесцветной пустоте небес.

1926

ПРОГУЛКА

У животных нет названья.
Кто им зваться повелел?
Равномерное страданье –
Их невидимый удел.

The sky is coming down to meet us here.
Our squishy bodies gradually harden,
Blood vessels stiffen blissfully,
And we can lift no more our sprouting feet
Or drop again our widely outspread arms.
Our eyes have closed, the time has fallen away,
And reaching tenderly, the sun touches our heads.

The waves of wetness course within our legs.
And now the moisture streaming upwards races
To wash and to refresh our leafy faces:
The earth caresses lovingly its offspring.
And in the distance streetlamps crowd like maces
Over the city, smouldering.

The city was a donkey, was a four-walled house.
It rolled along the dense horizon
On its two heavy wheels of stone,
Dry smokestacks sailing at a heel.
The day was full of light. The hollow clouds
Kept popping out and flew like wrinkled bubbles.
Wind went around the forest edge.
And there we stood, the long and slender trees,
In the pale blankness of the skies.

   1926

A WALK

Animals are nameless creatures.
Who decreed they bear a name?
Toils untold, unnoticed tortures –
Evenly their lot's the same.

Бык, беседуя с природой,
Удаляется в луга.
Над прекрасными глазами
Светят белые рога.
Речка девочкой невзрачной
Притаилась между трав,
То смеется, то рыдает,
Ноги в землю закопав.
Что же плачет? Что тоскует?
Отчего она больна?
Вся природа улыбнулась
Как высокая тюрьма.
Каждый маленький цветочек
Машет маленькой рукой.
Бык седые слезы точит,
Ходит пышный, чуть живой.
А на воздухе пустынном
Птица легкая кружится,
Ради песенки старинной
Нежным горлышком трудится.
Перед ней сияют воды,
Лес качается велик,
И смеется вся природа,
Умирая каждый миг.

1929

ИСКУШЕНИЕ

Смерть приходит к человеку,
Говорит ему: "Хозяин,
Ты походишь на калеку,
Насекомыми кусаем.

In a colloquy with nature
A bull withdraws to meadowlands,
And above his eyes of beauty
His white horns exalted stand.
Feet all buried underground,
A river hides amid the grass,
Now she laughs and now she whimpers,
Like a homely country lass.
Why the weeping? Why the tears?
What has gone with her so wrong?
All of nature lights up smiling,
Like a prison, tall and strong.
Every pretty little flower
Waves its pretty little arm.
And the bull sheds hoary tears,
Lush, and weary, and alarmed.
And on the deserted air
An easy songbird wheels about,
Working on an olden air
With its gentle, tiny throat.
Water shines in sunny weather,
The forest reaches to the skies,
All of nature laughs together,
And in every instant dies.

   1929

TEMPTATION

Death comes to a man unbidden,
Says to him: "Hey, listen, peasant,
You're a ruined, insect-bitten
Cripple, all-around unpleasant.

Брось житье, иди за мною,
У меня во гробе тихо.
Белым саваном укрою
Всех от мала до велика.
Не грусти, что будет яма,
Что с тобой умрет наука:
Поле выпашется само,
Рожь поднимется без плуга.
Солнце в полдень будет жгучим,
Ближе к вечеру прохладным.
Ты же, опытом научен,
Будешь белым и могучим
С медным крестиком квадратным
Спать во гробе аккуратном."

"Смерть, хозяина не трогай, –
Отвечает ей мужик. –
Ради старости убогой
Пощади меня на миг.
Дай мне малую отсрочку,
Отпусти меня. А там
Я единственную дочку
За труды тебе отдам."

Смерть не плачет, не смеется,
В руки девицу берет
И, как полымя, несется,
И трава под нею гнется
От избушки до ворот.

Холмик во поле стоит,
Дева в холмике шумит:
"Тяжело лежать во гробе,
Почернели ручки обе,
Стали волосы как пыль,
Из грудей растет ковыль.

In my coffin there's no trouble,
Quit your living, come with me.
Young or old, I'll have you cuddled
In a white shroud cosily.
Don't sweat over the pit and stone,
Don't regret your dying lore:
Fields will get tilled on their own,
Rye unsown will rise once more.
And the midday will burn bright,
And the evening will be blessed.
Meanwhile, you will close your eyes,
Sleeping, mighty, pale and wise.
In a tidy grave, you'll rest
With a brass cross on your chest."

"Death, have mercy on the ploughman –
Says the man – give me a break,
Pass me over for a moment
For my wretched age's sake.
Just come back a little later,
Let me off the hook today.
You can take my only daughter
For your labours right away."

Never laughing, never weeping,
Death picks up the girl and straight
Through the farmyard dashes, sweeping
All the grass behind it, leaping
From the hut and to the gate.

There's a hillock in the leas,
There's a maiden making pleas
In the grave: "It's dim and dank,
My wee hands turned black and shrank,
My fair hair has gone to bits,
Feather-grass grows from my tits.

Тяжело лежать в могиле,
Губки тоненькие сгнили,
Вместо глазок – два кружка,
Нету милого дружка!"

Смерть над холмиком летает
И хохочет и грустит,
Из ружья в него стреляет
И склоняясь, говорит:
"Ну, малютка, полно врать,
Полно в гробе глотку драть!
Мир над миром существует,
Вылезай из гроба прочь!
Слышишь, ветер в поле дует,
Наступает снова ночь.
Караваны сонных звезд
Пролетели, пронеслись.
Кончен твой подземный пост,
Ну, попробуй, поднимись!"

Дева ручками взмахнула,
Не поверила ушам,
Доску вышибла, вспрыгнула,
Хлоп! И лопнула по швам.

И течет, течет бедняжка
В виде маленьких кишок.
Где была ее рубашка,
Там остался порошок.
Изо всех отверстий тела
Червяки глядят несмело,
Вроде маленьких малют
Жидкость розовую пьют.

Была дева – стали щи.
Смех, не смейся, подожди!

Lying in the grave's a chore,
My fine lips all rot and gore,
Eyes forgot the light of day,
And my sweetheart's far away!"

Death comes flying to the spot,
Ever sorrowful and merry,
Fires at it a charge of shot,
Bends to her and says: "Look, cherry,
Stop already, cut this guff
From the pit, enough's enough!
There's a world above the world,
Get yourself out of the shadows!
Hear the wailing wind there, girl,
Night is falling on the meadows.
Caravans of stars amassed
Sweeping through the sleepy skies.
End your subterranean fast,
Come now, get yourself to rise!"

And the maid flings her hands up,
Can't believe it's not a dream,
Pushes, bursts the board, stands up,
"Pop!" – and splits along the seams.

All she had she spills, poor thing,
In a stream of tiny guts.
Where her shirt was fluttering,
There's a smattering of dust.
From her body's every spout
Little worms are peeking out,
Each one like a teensy ripper
Winks and drinks the pinkish liquor.

Here's a maid turned cabbage soup.
Laughter, stop the laughing, stop!

Солнце встанет, глина треснет,
Мигом девица воскреснет.
Из берцовой из кости
Будет деревце расти,
Будет деревце шуметь,
Про девицу песни петь,
Про девицу песни петь,
Сладким голосом звенеть:

"Баю, баюшки, баю,
Баю девочку мою!
Ветер в поле улетел,
Месяц в небе побелел.
Мужики по избам спят,
У них много есть котят.
А у каждого кота
Были красны ворота,
Шубки синеньки у них,
Все в сапожках золотых,
Все в сапожках золотых,
Очень, очень дорогих…"

1929

МЕРКНУТ ЗНАКИ ЗОДИАКА

Меркнут знаки Зодиака
Над просторами полей.
Спит животное Собака,
Дремлет птица Воробей.
Толстозадые русалки
Улетают прямо в небо,
Руки крепкие, как палки,

The sun will rise, the clay will crack,
And the maid will come right back.
From her shinbone through the clay
A sapling tree will spring one day,
It will grow so tall and strong,
It will sing the maid a song,
It will sing the maid a song,
Sweetly chiming all night long:

"Hush ye baby, hush-a-bye,
Hush ye baby, do not cry!
Gone's the wind to roam the vale,
In the sky, the moon's turned pale.
In their log huts peasants sleep,
Their cats meow and kittens peep.
All their kittens, all their cats
Wear fur coats and scarlet hats,
Their blue mittens are double-rolled,
They have pretty boots of gold,
They have pretty boots of gold,
Precious boots of price untold…"

   1929

ZODIAC SIGNS

Zodiac signs grow dim and narrow,
Over the fields in rising fog.
Sleep comes to the bird called Sparrow
And the animal called Dog.
Merry mermaids, nice and plump,
Soar up high above the ground,
Arms like clubs and hefty rump,

Груди круглые, как репа.
Ведьма, сев на треугольник,
Превращается в дымок.
С лешачихами покойник
Стройно пляшет кекуок.
Вслед за ними бледным хором
Ловят Муху колдуны,
И стоит над косогором
Неподвижный лик луны.

Меркнут знаки Зодиака
Над постройками села,
Спит животное Собака,
Дремлет рыба Камбала,
Колотушка тук-тук-тук,
Спит животное Паук,
Спит Корова, Муха спит,
Над землей луна висит.
Над землей большая плошка
Опрокинутой воды.
Леший вытащил бревешко
Из мохнатой бороды.
Из-за облака сирена
Ножку выставила вниз,
Людоед у джентльмена
Неприличное отгрыз.
Все смешалось в общем танце,
И летят во все концы
Гамадрилы и британцы,
Ведьмы, блохи, мертвецы.

Кандидат былых столетий,
Полководец новых лет,
Разум мой! Уродцы эти —
Только вымысел и бред.
Только вымысел, мечтанье,

Breasts like turnips, firm and round.
A witch straddles a triangle
And turns to smoke with a loud clap.
Goblin-ladies in a tangle
With a dead man trot and tap.
Ghostly sorcerers on the hill
Chase the Fly in a circle dance,
And above them hanging still
Is the moon's pale countenance.

Zodiac signs grow dim and narrow
Up above the village street.
Sleep comes to the bird called Sparrow,
And the vegetable called Beet.
Watchman's clapper goes rat-tat,
Sleep comes to the beast called Cat,
Spider sleeps, Cow's lost in dreams,
In the sky the moon-face gleams.
In the sky an earthen bowl,
Full of upturned water, floats.
Look: a wood-gnome pulls a pole
From his bushy beard and gloats.
Look: a siren from the cloud
Shows her pretty little foot,
And an ogre gnaws the lewd
Bit off a dandy, with a hoot.
Everything cavorts and riots,
Flutters all around and flits:
Cadavers and hamadryads,
Witches, spiders, fleas and Brits.

Candidate of bygone eras,
Captain of the years to come,
My wretched mind – these wild chimeras
Are just nightmares, worthless scum!
Only nightmares, hallucinations,

Сонной мысли колыханье,
Безутешное страданье, –
То, чего на свете нет.

Высока земли обитель.
Поздно, поздно. Спать пора!
Разум, бедный мой воитель,
Ты заснул бы до утра.
Что сомненья? Что тревоги?
День прошел, и мы с тобой –
Полузвери, полубоги –
Засыпаем на пороге
Новой жизни молодой.

Колотушка тук-тук-тук,
Спит животное Паук,
Спит Корова, Муха спит,
Над землей луна висит.
Над землей большая плошка
Опрокинутой воды.
Спит растение Картошка.
Засыпай скорей и ты!

1929

ИСКУССТВО

Дерево растет, напоминая
Естественную деревянную колонну.
От нее расходятся члены,
Одетые в круглые листья.
Собранье таких деревьев
Образует лес, дубраву.

Drowsy reason's undulations,
Inconsolable tribulations,
Fictions, shadowy and glum.

Lofty is this earthly dwelling.
Tireless warrior, my restless mind,
Go to sleep, there's no foretelling,
Let us leave the day behind!
It is gone, the troubles have ceased,
Why the doubts and why the strife?
We're part deity, part beast,
We shall sleep until we feast
With a new and youthful life.

Watchman's clapper goes rat-tat,
Dreams come to the beast called Cat,
Spider sleeps, Cow's lost in dreams,
In the sky the moon-face gleams.
In the sky an earthen bowl,
Full of upturned water, glows.
Sleep comes to the fish called Sole,
So your weary eyes shall close.

   1929

ART

A living tree is reminiscent
Of a natural wooden column.
It sprouts outstretched members
Dressed in circular leaves.
A congregation of such trees
Constitutes a grove, a forest.

Но определенье леса неточно,
Если указать на одно формальное строенье.

Толстое тело коровы,
Поставленное на четыре окончанья,
Увенчанное хромовидной головою
И двумя рогами (словно луна в первой четверти),
Тоже будет непонятно,
Также будет непостижимо,
Если забудем о его значенье
На карте живущих всего мира.

Дом, деревянная постройка,
Составленная как кладбище деревьев,
Сложенная, как шалаш из трупов,
Словно беседка из мертвецов, –
Кому он из смертных понятен,
Кому из живущих доступен,
Если забудем человека,
Кто строил его и рубил?

Человек, владыка планеты,
Государь деревянного леса,
Император коровьего мяса,
Саваоф двухэтажного дома, –
Он и планетою правит,
Он и леса вырубает,
Он и корову зарежет,
А вымолвить слова не может.

Но я, однообразный человек,
Взял в рот длинную сияющую дудку,
Дул, и подчиненные дыханию,
Слова вылетали в мир, становясь предметами.
Корова мне кашу варила,
Дерево сказку читало,

But the forest definition is lacking
If it only indicates the formal structure.

A cow's portly body
Established on four extremities,
Crowned with a calfskin head
And two horns (like a first quarter moon)
Will too remain a puzzle,
Will also be unfathomable,
If we forget its significance
On the map of all that lives in the world.

A house, a wooden edifice,
Constructed as a graveyard of trees,
Composed like a shelter out of corpses,
A gazebo out of dead bodies –
Which mortal can comprehend it,
Who of the living can grasp it,
If we forget about
The man who cut it and built it?

Man, the ruler of the planet,
The sovereign of the wooden forest,
The emperor of the flesh of the cow
Lord Almighty of the two-story building, –
He who reigns over the planet,
He who cuts the forest,
He who slaughters the cow,
Not a word can he utter.

But I, an indistinguishable man,
Put to my lips an elongated shining reedpipe
And blew, and subject to my breath,
Words flew out in the world and turned into things.
The cow made pottage for me,
The tree read me a fairy tale,

А мертвые домики мира
Прыгали, словно живые.

1930

ВРЕМЯ

1

Ираклий, Тихон, Лев, Фома
Сидели важно вкруг стола.
Над ними дедовский фонарь
Висел, роняя свет на пир.
Фонарь был важный и старинный,
Но в виде женщины чугунной.
Та женщина висела на цепях,
Ей в спину наливали масла,
Дабы лампада не погасла
И не остаться всем впотьмах.

2

Благообразная вокруг
Сияла комната для пира.
У стен – с провизией сундук,
Там – изображение кумира
Из дорогого алебастра.
В горшке цвела большая астра.
И несколько стульев прекрасных
Вокруг стояли стен однообразных.

And the dead huts of the world
Hopped like they were alive.

    1930

TIME

    1

Irakly, Tikhon, Leo and Tom
Around the table sat with pomp.
Above them, a grandfather lamp
Hung, dropping festive light on them.
The lamp was old and very splendid,
But shaped like a cast-iron lady
Suspended on a chain, massive and stark.
On her backside she had a spout
For oil, so light would not go out,
And they would not be left in dark.

    2

All ready for a glorious feast,
A handsome room around them shone
Where standing by the wall a chest
With various victuals bore a stone
Effigy of precious alabaster,
And in a pot, a blooming aster.
And several beautiful chairs
Along the bare walls stood in pairs.

3

Так в этой комнате жилой
Сидело четверо пирующих гостей.
Иногда они вскакивали,
Хватались за ножки своих бокалов
И пронзительно кричали "Виват!"
Светила лампа в двести ватт.
Ираклий был лесной солдат,
Имел ружья огромную тетерю,
В тетере был большой курок.
Нажав его перстом, я верю,
Животных бить возможно впрок.

4

Ираклий говорил, изображая
Собой могучую фигуру:
"Я женщин с детства обожаю.
Они представляют собой роскошную клавиатуру,
Из которой можно извлекать аккорды."
Со стен смотрели морды
Животных, убитых во время перестрелки.
Часы двигали свои стрелки.
И не сдержав разбег ума,
Сказал задумчивый Фома:
"Да, женщины значение огромно,
Я в том согласен безусловно,
Но мысль о времени сильнее женщин. Да!
Споем песенку о времени, которую мы поем всегда."

3

So in these living quarters
Four guests were gathered for a celebration.
Sometimes they sprang up from their seats,
Grabbed the stems of their glasses
And shouted strident *vivats*.
The lamp blazed at two hundred watts.
Irakly, a soldier of the woods,
Owned a huge turkey of a gun,
Which turkey had a clever trigger.
By pulling it, I gather, one
Could shoot wild animals with vigour.

4

Irakly rose with stature and acumen
To give a speech, and so it went:
"Since childhood I adored all women.
They are akin to a luxurious musical instrument
On which one can strike a chord."
Heads, mounted on a board,
Of hunting trophy animals, looked from the wall.
Clock hands continued with their crawl.
Unable to hold back the stride
Of thought, the pensive Tom replied:
"Indeed! I totally support your stance
On women's huge significance,
And yet, the thought of time grips stronger than they. Shall
We now sing our little ditty about time, as usual?"

5 Песенка о времени

Легкий ток из чаши А
Тихо льется в чашу Бе,
Вяжет дева кружева,
Пляшут звезды на трубе.

Поворачивая ввысь
Андромеду и Коня,
Над землею поднялись
Кучи звездного огня.

Год за годом, день за днем
Звездным мы горим огнем,
Плачем мы, созвездий дети,
Тянем руки к Андромеде

И уходим навсегда,
Увидавши, как в трубе
Легкий ток из чаши А
Тихо льется в чашу Бе.

6

Тогда ударил вновь бокал
И снова все "Виват!" вскричали,
И им в ответ, устроив бал,
Часы пять криков прокричали.
Как будто маленький собор,
Висящий крепко на гвозде,
Часы кричали с давних пор,
Как надо двигаться звезде.
Бездонный времени сундук,
Часы – творенье адских рук!

5 A Song about Time

A dreamy stream from vessel A
Trickles down to vessel B,
Maidens weave the lace all day,
Stars dance nightly in the tree.

Piles of shining starlight churn
In the heavens on their course,
They climb the firmament and turn
Round Andromeda and the Horse.

Day by day and year by year
We're consumed with starlight here,
Children of the stars, we cry
To Andromeda up high

And forever go away,
When we suddenly can see
A dreamy stream from vessel A
Trickling down to vessel B.

6

All cheered again in unity,
And glasses clinked once more and rose,
And in response, like a maître d',
The clock crowed five cries in a row.
A small cathedral on the wall,
Hung firmly on an iron nail,
From ancient times, the clock's loud call
Directed where the stars must sail.
A time chest, an abyssal well –
The clock is but a work of hell!

И все это прекрасно понимая,
Сказал Фома, родиться мысли помогая:
"Я предложил бы истребить часы",
И закрутив усы,
Он посмотрел на всех спокойным глазом.
Блестела женщина своим чугунным тазом.

7

А если бы они взглянули за окно,
Они б увидели великое пятно
Вечернего светила.
Растенья там росли, как дудки,
Цветы качались выше плеч,
И в каждой травке, как в желудке,
Возможно свету было течь.
Мясных растений городок
Пересекал воды поток.
И, обнаженные, слагались
В ладошки длинные листы,
И жилы нижние купались
Среди химической воды.

8

И с отвращеньем посмотрев в окошко.
Сказал Фома: «Ни клюква, ни морошка,
Ни жук, ни мельница ни пташка,
Ни женщины большая ляжка
Меня не радуют. Имейте все в виду:
Часы стучат, и я сейчас уйду».

9

Тогда встает безмолвный Лев,
Ружье берет, остервенев,

And seeing it for what it's truly worth,
Tom said, as if he helped his thought emerge from birth:
"I would propose to extirpate the clock",
And with a tranquil look
He glanced at others twisting his moustache.
The woman lightly swayed, her iron haunches flashed.

7

But if they looked out of the window, they could watch
The evening sun's gigantic sinking blotch
On the horizon.
Plants grew like panpipes full of music,
Their flowers swayed at shoulder height,
And every stalk was like a stomach,
An easy conduit for light.
A water stream ran through a city
Of vegetation, soft and meaty.
The elongated leaves, stark naked,
Folded like hands on every tree,
And lower tendons bathed amid
The flowing water's chemistry.

8

Tom glanced out of the window with disgust
And said: "I'm tired of the female bust,
The beetle's buzz, the bird's shrill trills;
Cloudberries, cranberries or mills
Don't make me happy. So, mind what you hear:
The clock is ticking, and I'm out of here."

9

Then Leo, in silent fury, stands
Up, takes a shotgun in his hands

Влагает в дуло два заряда,
Всыпает порох роковой
И в середину циферблата
Стреляет крепкою рукой.
И все в дыму стоят, как боги,
И шепчут, грозные: «Виват!»
И женщины железной ноги
Горят над ними в двести ватт.
И все растенья припадают
К стеклу, похожему на клей,
И с удивленьем наблюдают
Могилу разума людей.

1933

ИСПЫТАНИЕ ВОЛИ

АГАФОНОВ
Прошу садиться, выпить чаю.
У нас варенья полон чан.

КОРНЕЕВ
Среди посуд я различаю
Прекрасный чайник англичан.

АГАФОНОВ
Твой глаз, Корнеев, навострился,
Ты видишь Англии фарфор.
Он в нашей келье появился
Еще совсем с недавних пор.
Мне подарил его мой друг
Открыв с посудою сундук.

And stuffs the barrels with two rounds,
His cheek pressed firmly to the stock,
Takes aim – a fateful shot resounds,
Straight in the centre of the clock.
Smoke swirls around them like an omen,
God-like, they whisper fierce *vivats,*
The big legs of the iron woman
Floodlight them at two hundred watts.
And all the vegetables gather
Close to the window, and from behind
The glue-like glass, observe in wonder
The graveyard of the human mind.

   1933

A TRIAL OF THE WILL

   AGAFONOV [*ah-guff-OH-nuff*]
Welcome, sit down and have some tea.
We have a wealth of jams on hand.

   KORNEEV [*car-NEIGH-off*]
Among your crockery I see
A fine teapot from British land.

   AGAFONOV
You are, Korneev, quite sharp-eyed,
You can discern fine English ware.
We only recently acquired
This teapot for our modest lair.
It is a friend's gift. He discovered
It on a back shelf in his cupboard.

КОРНЕЕВ

Невероятна речь твоя,
Приятель сердца Агафонов!
Ужель могу поверить я:
Предмет, достойный Пантеонов,
Роскошный Англии призрак,
Который видом тешит зрак,
Жжет душу, разум просветляет,
Больных к художеству склоняет,
Засохшим сердце веселит,
А сам сияет и горит, –
Ужель такой предмет высокий,
Достойный лучшего венца,
Отныне в хижине убогой
Травою лечит мудреца?

АГАФОНОВ

Да, это правда.

КОРНЕЕВ
                        Боже правый!
Предмет, достойный лучших мест,
Стоит, наполненный отравой,
Где Агафонов кашу ест!
Подумай только: среди ручек,
Которы тонки, как зефир,
Он мог бы жить в условьях лучших
И почитаться как кумир.
Властитель Англии туманной,
Его поставивши в углу,
Сидел бы весь благоуханный,
Шепча посуде похвалу.
Наследник пышною особой
При нем ходил бы, сняв сапог,
И в виде милости особой
Его за носик трогать мог.

KORNEEV

What is it that I hear from you,
My dearest soulmate Agafonov!
Can I believe that it is true?
A piece fit for the Pantheon, of
The English a luxurious ghost,
A piece that holds one's eyes engrossed,
That clears the mind and burns the heart,
Disposes the infirm to art,
Brings merriment to hardened souls,
That brightly shines and warmly glows –
Does this exalted artefact
Worthy of taking centre stage,
Reside now in this wretched shack
To steep a potion for a sage?

AGAFONOV

Yes, it is true.

KORNEEV

          O Goodness gracious!
An object fit for kings, no less,
Stands filled with tea, a bane herbaceous,
Where Agafonov eats his mess!
Just think: among the fairest hands
As thin as zephyr, nobly idle,
It could have lived in better lands,
Revered and cherished like an idol.
The ruler of the foggy Britain
Would put it in an honoured spot
And sit wrapped in a perfumed chiton
Whispering praises to the pot.
His heir, a very sumptuous person,
Would saunter shoeless in bare toes
Imploring for a kind permission
To merely touch it on the nose.

И вдруг такие небылицы!
В простую хижину упав,
Сей чайник носит нам водицы,
Хотя не князь ты и не граф.

АГАФОНОВ
Среди различных лицедеев
Я слышал множество похвал,
Но от тебя, мой друг Корнеев,
Таких речей не ожидал.
Ты судишь, право, как лунатик,
Ты весь от страсти изнемог,
И жила вздулась, как канатик,
Обезобразив твой висок.
Ужели чайник есть причина?
Возьми его! На что он мне!

КОРНЕЕВ
Благодарю тебя, мужчина.
Теперь спокоен я вполне.
Прощай. Я все еще рыдаю.
(Уходит)

АГАФОНОВ
Я духом в воздухе летаю,
Я телом в келейке лежу
И чайник снова в келью приглашу.

КОРНЕЕВ
(входит)

Возьми обратно этот чайник,
Он ненавистен мне навек:
Я был премудрости начальник,
А стал пропащий человек.

But this is patently absurd:
This teapot serves us as a fount
Onto your wretched hut conferred,
Though you are neither prince nor count!

AGAFONOV
Between the hypocrite and knave
I have in every way been praised,
But your words, dearest friend Korneev,
I have to say, leave me amazed.
You are so passionate you tremble,
You argue like a lunatic,
An ugly vein across your temple
Is bulging in a nervous tic –
A tempest in a teapot brewed.
Take it! What use is it for me?

KORNEEV
You have, good sir, my gratitude.
Now I've attained tranquillity.
Farewell to you. I'm still in tears.
    (Exits)

AGAFONOV
I let my soul soar in the spheres,
I rest my body on the cot,
And I shall shortly summon back the pot.

KORNEEV
    (Enters)

Take back from me this cursed crock,
I hate it fiercely, take it back.
I used to be a sage, a warlock,
And now I'm but a wretched wreck.

АГАФОНОВ
(обнимая его)

Хвала тебе, мой друг Корнеев,
Ты чайник духом победил.
Итак, бери его скорее:
Я дарю тебе его изо всех сил.

1931

ОТДЫХ

Вот на площади квадратной
Маслодельня, белый дом!
Бык гуляет аккуратный,
Чуть качая животом.
Дремлет кот на белом стуле,
Под окошком вьются гули,
Бродит тетя Мариули,
Звонко хлопая ведром.

Сепаратор, бог чухонский.
Масла розовый король!
Укроти свой топот конский,
Полюбить тебя позволь.
Дай мне два кувшина сливок,
Дай сметаны полведра,
Чтобы пел я возле ивок
Вплоть до самого утра!

Маслодельни легкий стук,
Масла маленький сундук,
Что стучишь ты возле пашен,
Там, где бык гуляет, важен,

AGAFONOV
(Hugs him)

Praise be to you, my friend Korneev,
Your spirit fought the pot and won.
Accept it as a gift, I pray you,
I present it to you with my full conviction.

   1931

LEISURE

At the squarish village square
Stands the whitewashed creamery.
A bull strolls there, neat and fair,
Its round belly swaying free.
On the chair a cat sleeps duly,
Pigeons wheel outside, unruly,
And sweet Auntie Mariuli
Clangs her bucket merrily.

Separator, god of Ingers,
Butter-king of ruddy hue!
Stop your horsey clop and jingle,
Let me fall in love with you.
Give me butter, half a bucket,
And two jugs of your sweet cream,
I'll be singing in the thicket
Till the morning's early beam!

Oh, the creamery's light clatter!
Little coffer full of butter,
What's the clacking all about
Where the bull walks, grand and stout?

125

Что играешь возле ив,
Стенку набок наклонив?

Спой мне, тетя Мариули,
Песню, легкую, как сон!
Все животные заснули,
Месяц в небо унесен.
Безобразный, конопатый,
Словно толстый херувим,
Дремлет дядя Волохатый
Перед домиком твоим.
Все спокойно. Вечер с нами!
Лишь на улице глухой
Слышу: бьется под ногами
Заглушенный голос мой.

1930

ПРЕДОСТЕРЕЖЕНИЕ

Где древней музыки фигуры,
Где с мертвым бой клавиатуры,
Где битва нот с безмолвием пространства –
Там не ищи, поэт, душе своей убранства.

Соединив безумие с умом,
Среди пустынных смыслов мы построим дом –
Училище миров, невиданных доселе.
Поэзия есть мысль, устроенная в теле.

What's the music that you chant
By the willows, walls aslant?

Sing me, Auntie Mariuli,
Sing your song, light as a dream!
All the feathered and the woolly
Fell asleep, the moon's agleam.
An enormous freckled fatty,
A cherub, hideous and rough,
Sleepy Uncle Volokhaty
By your cottage dozes off.
All is calm! The night is ours.
Still, I can't but hear my mute
Voice at this forsaken hour
Beating, trampled underfoot.

  1930

A FOREWARNING

Where shapes of ancient music form,
Where keyboard takes dead men by storm,
Where notes attack the silence of the space –
Seek not garb for your soul*, O poet, in that place.

We'll harness folly side by side with wisdom,
Among deserted meanings we shall build a home,
A school for worlds unseen, unusual and fresh.
For poetry is thought established in the flesh.

* A reference to Seneca's Epistle CXV: 'Oratio cultus animi est' (Speech
is the garb of the soul). Thus, Zabolotsky states that music / musicality
should not be a feature of poetic speech, perhaps in direct polemic with
Verlaine's 'Ars Poetica' ("De la musique avant toute chose")..

Она течет, незримая, в воде –
Мы воду воспоем усердными трудами,
Она горит в полуночной звезде –
Звезда, как полымя, бушует перед нами.

Тревожный сон коров и беглый разум птиц
Пусть смотрят из твоих диковинных страниц.
Деревья пусть поют и страшным разговором
Пугает бык людей, тот самый бык, в котором
Заключено безмолвие миров,
Соединенных с нами крепкой связью.

Побит камнями и закидан грязью,
Будь терпелив. И помни каждый миг:
Коль музыки коснешься чутким ухом,
Разрушится твой дом и, ревностный к наукам,
Над нами посмеется ученик.

1932

ОТДЫХАЮЩИЕ КРЕСТЬЯНЕ

Толпа высоких мужиков
Сидела важно на бревне.
Обычай жизни был таков,
Досуги, милые вдвойне.
Царя ли свергнут или разом
Скотину волк на поле съест,
Они сидят, гуторя басом,
Про то да се узнав окрест.
Иногда во тьме ночной
Приносят длинную гармошку,
Извлекают резкие продолжительные звуки

And if it flows, invisible, in water –
We'll labour earnestly to sing the water's praise,
And if it burns inside a midnight star –
We'll keep our eyes on the star's raging blaze.

Let cow's uneasy sleep and fluent mind of birds
Stare at the readers from your odd and quirky words.
And let the trees sing, let the bull scare people away
With terrifying talk; the bull that holds the sway
Of worlds immersed in tranquil soundlessness,
Connected to us with a lasting bond.

And when you find yourself mud-smeared and stoned,
Be patient. And remember all the while:
If you allow your ear a brush with music, then
Your house will fall apart, and students, keen to learn,
Will look at us with but a bitter smile.

   1932

PEASANTS AT LEISURE

A crowd of stately village men
Sat on a log with a pompous air.
Such was the life's sweet habit then,
Unhurried leisure, time to spare.
Whether the tsar's been overthrown
Or wolves have taken all the herd,
They'd sit with dignity and drone
About what everyone has heard.
Sometimes, when the night is dark,
They bring an oblong concertina,
Elicit from it protracted, high-pitched sounds

И на травке молодой
Скачут страшными прыжками,
Взявшись за руки, толпой.
Вот толпа несется, воет,
Слышен запах потной кожи,
Музыканты рожи строят,
На чертей весьма похожи.
В громе, давке, кувырканье
"Эх, пошла! – кричат. – Наддай-ка!"
Реют бороды бараньи,
Стонет, воет балалайка.
"Эх, пошла!" И дым столбом,
От натуги бледны лица.
Многоногий пляшет ком,
Воет, стонет, веселится.
Но старцы сумрачной толпой
Сидят на бревнах меж домами,
И лунный свет, виясь столбами,
Висит над ними как живой.
Тогда, привязанные к хатам,
Они глядят на этот мир,
Обсуждают, что такое атом,
Каков над воздухом эфир.
И скажет кто-нибудь, печалясь,
Что мы, пожалуй, не цари,
Что наверху плывут, качаясь,
Миров иные кубари.
Гром мечут, искры составляют,
Живых растеньями питают,
А мы, приклеены к земле,
Сидим, как птенчики в дупле.
Тогда крестьяне, созерцая
Природы стройные холмы,
Сидят, задумчиво мерцая
Глазами страшной старины.
Иной жуков наловит в шапку,

And upon the new, green grass
Make their fearsome leaps and bounds
Holding hands, a solid mass.
Now the wild crowd howls and races,
The air is full of sweaty skin,
And musicians making faces
Look like demons in the din.
In the ruckus, jumble, roar
"Kick 'er up!" – they shout – "Go bonkers!"
Beards of sheepskin flit and soar,
Balalaika screams and whimpers.
"Kick 'er up!" – All stops are out
A many-footed dancing blob –
Faces pale with effort – shouts,
Howls in merriment, and sobs.
But then, amid the swirling hive
Old men sit on the logs, all sombre,
And moonlight twists like beams of timber
Over their heads, as if alive.
Tied to their huts, they try to fathom
The world at which they keenly stare,
They discuss the nature of the atom,
What ether's like above the air.
And someone says, wistful and bitter,
That there are kings, but we are slaves,
And other worlds that up there glitter
Are spinning tops on ether waves.
They gather firesparks, they throw thunder,
Nourish with plants those who live under,
While glued onto the surface, we
Sit there like nestlings in the tree.
Then peasants peacefully observing
The shapely hills that nature raised,
Sit with their eyes gleaming with fervent
And frightful fire of ancient days.
And one would catch bugs with his hat

Глядит, внимателен и тих,
Какие есть у тварей лапки,
Какие крылышки у них.
Иной первоначальный астроном
Слагает из бересты телескоп,
И ворон с каменным крылом
Стоит на крыше, словно поп.
А на вершинах Зодиака,
Где слышен музыки орган,
Двенадцать люстр плывут из мрака,
Составив круглый караван.
И мы под ними, как малютки,
Сидим, считая день за днем,
И, в кучу складывая сутки,
Весь месяц в люстру отдаем.

1933

БИТВА СЛОНОВ

Воин слова, по ночам
Петь пора твоим мечам!

На бессильные фигурки существительных
Кидаются лошади прилагательных,
Косматые всадники
Преследуют конницу глаголов,
И снаряды междометий
Рвутся над головами,
Как сигнальные ракеты.

Битва слов! Значений бой!
В башне Синтаксис – разбой.

And watch with mind intent and quiet
What kind of legs the creature has,
What kind of wings it has to fly it.
A primal stargazer, one toils alone
To build a telescope out of birch bast,
A raven stands, wings cast in stone,
Upon a rooftop, like a priest.
And at the heights of Zodiac,
Up where the music's organ sounds,
Twelve chandeliers float in the black,
A caravan on endless rounds.
And we, like little kids at play,
We're keeping count of days down here
And piling up day after day,
We give each month its chandelier.

1933

A BATTLE OF ELEPHANTS

Warriors of words, it's time
For your swords to sing and chime!

The horses of adjectives career towards
The feeble figures of common nouns,
Shaggy horsemen
Pursue the cavalry of verbs,
And interjection shells
Explode overhead
Like signal flares.

Words in battle! Senses clash!
The Syntax tower is burned and trashed.

Европа сознания
В пожаре восстания.
Невзирая на пушки врагов,
Стреляющие разбитыми буквами,
Боевые слоны подсознания
Вылезают и топчутся,
Словно исполинские малютки.

Но вот, с рождения не евши,
Они бросаются в таинственные бреши
И с человечьими фигурками в зубах
Счастливо поднимаются на задние ноги.
Слоны подсознания!
Боевые животные преисподней!
Они стоят, приветствуя веселым воем
Все, что захвачено разбоем.

Маленькие глазки слонов
Наполнены смехом и радостью.
Сколько игрушек! Сколько хлопушек!
Пушки замолкли, крови покушав,
Синтаксис домики строит не те,
Мир в неуклюжей стоит красоте.
Деревьев отброшены старые правила,
На новую землю их битва направила.
Они разговаривают, пишут сочинения,
Весь мир неуклюжего полон значения!
Волк вместо разбитой морды
Приделал себе человечье лицо,
Вытащил флейту, играет без слов
Первую песню военных слонов.

Поэзия, сраженье проиграв,
Стоит в растерзанной короне.
Рушились башен столетних Монбланы,
Где цифры сияли, как будто полканы,

The Europe of conscious elocution
Is ablaze with revolution.
In the face of enemy guns
Shooting volleys of broken letters,
The war elephants of the subconscious
Emerge and trample
Like gargantuan babies.

Unfed from birth, the hungry creatures
Rush headlong into the mysterious breaches
And happily rise up on their hind legs
With little human figures dangling from their teeth.
Elephants of the subconscious!
The battle animals of the netherworld!
They stand and hail with merry hoot
Everything they took as loot.

The elephants' little eyes
Fill with laughter and happiness.
Oh, what fun! These toys are best!
Blood-fed guns can go to rest.
Syntax builds houses that aren't quite right,
The world is an awkwardly beautiful sight.
The old rules for trees have been tossed overboard,
They march for new territories claimed by the sword.
They engage in conversations, they compose essays,
The world moves in clumsily meaningful ways!
Instead of his smashed, bloody snout
The wolf fixed himself a human face,
Pulled a flute out and plays the triumphant
Primal war chant of battle elephants.

Poetry has lost the battle
And stands there, its crown torn to shreds.
The mountainous towers are in ruins and cinders,
Where ciphers for centuries sparkled like centaurs,

Где меч силлогизма горел и сверкал,
Проверенный чистым рассудком.
И что же? Сражение он проиграл
Во славу иным прибауткам!

Поэзия в великой муке
Ломает бешеные руки,
Клянет весь мир,
Себя зарезать хочет,
То, как безумная, хохочет,
То в поле бросится, то вдруг
Лежит в пыли, имея много мук.
На самом деле, как могло случиться,
Что пала древняя столица?
Весь мир к поэзии привык,
Все было так понятно.
В порядке конница стояла,
На пушках цифры малевала,
И на знаменах слово Ум
Кивало всем, как добрый кум.
И вдруг какие-то слоны,
И все перевернулось!

Поэзия начинает приглядываться,
Изучать движение новых фигур,
Она начинает понимать красоту неуклюжести,
Красоту слона, выброшенного преисподней.

Сраженье кончено. В пыли
Цветут растения земли,
И слон, рассудком приручаем,
Ест пироги и запивает чаем.

   1931

Where the syllogism sword shone with brilliant light,
Its blade by pure reason enabled.
And what do you know? It has lost its big fight –
More glory to different fables!

Poetry wrings her livid arms
Blaming the whole world for the harms
She suffered,
She wants to stab herself,
She's like a madman: now she laughs,
Now runs away into the woods,
Now hits the dust in agony, and broods.
But come to think of it, how was it possible
For it to fall, the ancient capital?
The world grew used to poetry,
Everything was so familiar.
The cavalry stood in encampments
And painted numbers on the cannons,
And from the banners, the word: Mind
Waved like an uncle, mild and kind.
But then some elephants come up
And everything's upended!

Poetry is looking closer,
She studies the moves of the new figures,
She begins to understand the beauty of the clumsy,
The beauty of the elephant ejected by the netherworld.

The fight is over. Flowers spring forth
From dust, the children of the earth.
By reason tamed, the elephant of war
Eats pies and drinks tea from a samovar.

   1931

137

NIKOLAI ALEKSEYEVICH ZABOLOTSKY was born in 1903 in what is now the city of Kazan and spent his early years in what later became the Republic of Mari El and the Kirov Oblast. In 1920, Zabolotsky moved to Moscow, enrolling simultaneously in the departments of medicine and philology at the Moscow State University, moving a year later to the Leningrad State Pedagogical Institute. He had already begun to write poetry, his main influences being the Futurist works of Vladimir Mayakovsky and Velimir Khlebnikov, the lyrical poems of Alexander Blok and Sergei Yesenin, and the art of Pavel Filonov and Marc Chagall. During this period, Zabolotsky met his future wife, E. V. Klykova.

In 1928, Zabolotsky, with Daniil Kharms and Alexander Vvedensky, founded the avant-garde group Oberiu (the group's acronym stood for 'The Association of Real Art') and, in 1929, his first book of poetry, *Columns* (Столбцы), was published followed, in 1937, by a second poetry collection.

In 1938, Zabolotsky fell victim to Joseph Stalin's 'Great Purge'; he was accused of taking part in a counter-revolutionary plot with other Leningrad writers and sentenced to five years in Siberia, a sentence that was prolonged until the end of the Second World War. He was finally released in 1945.

Upon his return to Moscow in 1946, Zabolotsky was readmitted to the Union of Soviet Writers and resumed his work as a translator (particularly of Georgian poets) and on his own poetry. The last few years of Zabolotsky's life were beset by illness and he died in Moscow in 1958.

DMITRI MANIN is a physicist, programmer, and translator of poetry. His translations from English and French into Russian have appeared in several book collections. His latest work is a complete translation of Ted Hughes' *Crow* (Jaromír Hladík Press, 2020) and Allen Ginsberg's *The Howl, Kaddish and Other Poems* (Podpisnye Izdaniya, 2021). His translations from Russian to English have been published in books and journals, including *Delos, Metamorphoses, The Cafe Review* and *Cardinal Points* among others, as well as in Maria Stepanova's *The Voice Over* (Cambridge University Press, 2021). His translation of a poem by Stepanova won first prize in 2017 Compass Award competition.

DARRA GOLDSTEIN is the Willcox B. and Harriet M. Adsit Professor of Russian, Emerita at Williams College and Founding Editor of *Gastronomica: The Journal of Food and Culture,* named the 2012 Publication of the Year by the James Beard Foundation. She has published widely on literature, culture, art, and cuisine and has organized several exhibitions, including *Graphic Design in the Mechanical Age* and *Feeding Desire: Design and the Tools of the Table, 1500-2005,* both at the Cooper Hewitt Smithsonian Design Museum. In addition to serving as Editor in Chief of the James Beard-nominated *Oxford Companion to Sugar and Sweets,* she is the author of six award-winning cookbooks.

Darra is Series Editor of *California Studies in Food and Culture* (University of California Press) and has consulted for the Council of Europe as part of an international group exploring ways in which food can be used to promote tolerance and diversity. She was the national spokesperson for Stolichnaya vodka when it was first introduced to the US. Darra did her undergraduate work at Vassar College and holds a PhD from Stanford University, where she wrote her dissertation on Zabolotsky. Her monograph on his poetry, *Nikolai Zabolotsky: Play for Mortal Stakes,* was published by Cambridge University Press in 1993.

She currently serves on the Kitchen Cabinet of the Smithsonian's National Museum of American History and on the Advisory Board of the Julia Child Foundation for Gastronomy and the Culinary Arts.